God's
Mysterious
Ways

JOSEPHINE TAFFY KUTHEMBAMWALE

WESTBOW®
PRESS
A DIVISION OF THOMAS NELSON
& ZONDERVAN

Scripture taken from the King James Version of the Bible.

Scripture taken from the Holy Bible, NEW INTERNATIONAL VERSION®.
Copyright © 1973, 1978, 1984 by Biblica, Inc. All rights reserved worldwide.
Used by permission. NEW INTERNATIONAL VERSION® and NIV® are
registered trademarks of Biblica, Inc. Use of either trademark for the offering
of goods or services requires the prior written consent of Biblica US, Inc.

WestBow Press books may be ordered through booksellers or by contacting:

WestBow Press
A Division of Thomas Nelson & Zondervan
1663 Liberty Drive
Bloomington, IN 47403
www.westbowpress.com
1 (866) 928-1240

ISBN: 978-1-4908-6349-8 (sc)
ISBN: 978-1-4908-6350-4 (hc)
ISBN: 978-1-4908-6348-1 (e)

Library of Congress Control Number: 2014922161

Printed in the United States of America.

WestBow Press rev. date: 01/06/2015

CONTENTS

Introduction: Cake vii

Chapter 1:   The Journey Has Begun 1
Chapter 2:   In God We Trust 12
Chapter 3:   Health with God 17
Chapter 4:   Word 29
Chapter 5:   Why the Devil Hides His Identity.....................32
Chapter 6:   Do Good Work to Honour God 41
Chapter 7:   God Promises 46
Chapter 8:   How Caring is Our God....................................52
Chapter 9:   When God Says Yes, Who Can Say No? 58
Chapter 10: Testimonies...61
Chapter 11: Do Not Judge as You Judge.............................. 68
Chapter 12: Are Visitors Welcomed In Our Homes?........... 72
Chapter 13: He is My Shepherd 82
Chapter 14: Does God Speak to His People..........................89

INTRODUTION

Cake

Psalms 34:8 O taste and see that the Lord is good: blessed is the man that trusteth in him. (*KJV*) This book will teach us to know that the Lord is good. As a baker I always bake cakes. One day I was baking a birthday cake. As usual I gathered all the ingredients then I started talking to myself that without baking powder the cake shall not be a cake. Likewise, without flour it shall change to something else. I wanted to bake the best cake ever and I used much additive such as vanilla, cocoa powder and nutmeg and so I worked hard to make it best and it worked. It came to a stage of decorating the cake and the garnishing was super. Instead of admiring the whole work, I was busy with the icing decoration on top of the cake. It reminds me of something in my heart, most of the times we appreciate things we treasurer most, indeed things we see. The icing of the cake is not the cake and the cake is more important than the icing. Imagine when the cake rots but the icing is still there looking appetizing, can we eat the cake? The answer is an obvious one, no we cannot. Most of us we judge things according to the appearance, many men liked a woman because of her appearance similarly, most ladies like a man because of what they have. Even church leaders are chosen because of what they have. 1 Samuel16:7 But the Lord said to Samuel, 'Do not consider his appearance or his height, for I have rejected him (NIV). The Lord does not look at things man looks at. Man looks at the outward appearance, but the Lord looks at the heart. This verse teaches us to ask God to help us to see what lies deep in a person. Thus; we should have an inner eye which God gave us. From this book we can learn the goodness of the Lord through His teaching.

There are good topics that shall draw us close to the Lord and know Him. Make a step to God now and see His goodness, the bible tells us blessed is the man who takes refuge from God. Be one of the blessed men in the way of seeking Him and learn from Him. God is good and He is still working on us, helping us and He wants us to be with Him forever and ever. There is a song which "says by and by we shall understand it by and by" and the other song is "we shall overcome someday." Indeed, we will overcome one day and we will be with our father in Heaven.

CHAPTER ONE

The Journey Has Begun....

Are we ready? May be I should ask the question like this-: Have you packed the luggage? Suppose you are in a train station, bus stop, airport, port, tram station or your own car. You are setting out on a long journey and you need to leave at a right time. When you are on the journey, actually a long journey like moving to a country with a different climate, indeed a place where even the taste of the food is different from the one you are used to. For such journeys we are always conscious and ready at the right time.

We are always prepared for worldly journey. However, are we ready or are we fully prepared for the journey to Heaven or we are tired of waiting? If we are ready for heaven why are we still busy with worldly pleasures? Why are we buying the stories the world tells us and purchasing things others tell us as valuable? We are tempted by saying like "Jesus is here," and "The world is ending," we are attracted by issues of politics and economics, for instance; the global warming, economic problems and globalization, or by fashion like plastic surgery and sex operations. Jesus says: "In my Father's house are many mansion: if it were not so, I would have told you. I go to prepare a place for you (John 14:2,KJV). Jesus is telling us that the place He is going to prepare for us is the place for everybody who choose Him and who are obedient to all things he taught. The journey has begun now and the owner of the journey is Jesus Himself, so if we live in this world in the same way He did, that means we are on the journey with Jesus.

Do we fear? We should not be afraid of those things which are happening now because they are signs of the times. And what we need to do is to be ready for the journey and never drawback; yes it should be forward ever, backwards never. Our God tells us 365 times in the Bible "do not fear for I am with you." And His promise endures forever. Jesus says: "and if I go and prepare a place for you, I will come back and take you to be with me that you also be where I am. And whither I go ye know, and the way ye know" (John 14:3-4KJV). Jesus assures us that when He goes to our Father's house and prepare place for us, He will come to take us where He is going. That means that right now Jesus is preparing a place hence we need to prepare our hearts as well. In other words, we need to prepare for ourselves because Jesus promised that there are abundant rooms so that each one of us will have enough space.

The choice is ours to say; "No Jesus do not bother to prepare a room for me because I am busy with the world." It is our duty to prepare our hearts to have rooms in heaven. John14:4 Jesus reminds us further that we know the way to the place He is going. Ah! Can this be a trickle? Why? What is the way? Jesus answered that question in John 14:6 which states, "Jesus saith unto him; I am the way, the truth, and the life: no man cometh unto the Father, but by me" (KJV). Jesus Himself is both the only way for our journey and its destination as well. If we live like Him, we will make it to our destination. In Jesus there is truth and life that make Him the only way for our journey. As followers of Christ, we need to follow in His steps. In a nutshell, we need to ask ourselves that: what would Jesus do if He were in a situation we are in that time. In that way we will live as Him.

Indeed Jesus is the way, the truth, and the life. Jesus conquers the grave giving us the sign that there will be no more death in the New Jerusalem. What He did was the truth. We need Christ to show us the way and to lead and teach us in this world so that should make it to Heaven.

ARE WE READY FOR THE KINGDOM OF GOD?

As Jesus started on his way, a man ran up to him and fell on his knees before him. "Good teacher," he asked, "what must I do to inherit eternal life?"

"Why do you call me good?" Jesus answered. "No one is good—except God alone. You know the commandments: You shall not murder, you shall not commit adultery, you shall not steal, you shall not give false testimony, you shall not defraud, honour your father and mother. "Teacher," he declared, "all these I have kept since I was a boy." Jesus looked at him and loved him. "One thing you lack," he said. "Go, sell everything you have and give to the poor, and you will have treasure in heaven. Then come, follow me." At this the man's face fell. He went away sad, because he had great wealth. Jesus looked around and said to his disciples, "How hard it is for the rich to enter the kingdom of God!" The disciples were amazed at his words. But Jesus said again, "Children, how hard it is to enter the kingdom of God! It is easier for a camel to go through the eye of a needle than for someone who is rich to enter the kingdom of God (MARK10:17-25 (NIV)."

First and far most, what did he wants from Jesus? He went to Jesus in humility and loyalty; he looked like he knew what he wanted. This becomes evident as he asked Jesus what to do in order to inherit heaven. And Jesus looked at him and told him to keep the Lord's commandments. The man responded to Jesus very wisely; that he had done that since he was born. Jesus knew everything about this man.

Even today Jesus knows us all. Thus; he knows our strengths and weaknesses as well. And Jesus loved this man a lot. May be you and I have not done what this man did; keeping all Ten Commandments of the Lord. May the Good Lord help us to keep all His Commandments from this time forth. But there was one thing lacking in the man; Jesus told him to go and give everything he had to the poor, so that he could inherit the kingdom of heaven. Then Jesus told him to come and follow Him. The man's countenance entailed that he could not do as instructed hence he went away.

Likewise, for us the question is whether we can leave all what we have and follow Jesus so as to inherit heaven. How it was for this man to leave everything for heaven's sake. To be precise, the man came from a royal family and his riches flowed from his inheritance. Inheritance is property received from the family and not just from anyone, it's like kingship. Similarly, he thought heaven was also something one was supposed to inherit no wonder his question. It has to be stressed that Jesus loved then man because he wanted to know how he could inherit the kingdom of God.

However, it was very sad news for the man to give all that he had because of Jesus. Certainly, it was hard for him to lose the property of his children and grandchildren in order to follow Jesus. How about us? Could you manage today to have Jesus and Jesus alone even if it means we will be nothing to the world? Could you leave your lovely family because of Jesus? Could you leave your wife or husband because of Jesus? Could we leave everything that is very important to us because of Jesus? Could we?

Jesus said at the end of those two verses that it was hard to enter into heaven. Indeed, it is hard if we have not yet accepted Jesus Christ as our Saviour. God wants us to leave everything just like Jesus Himself did; He sacrificed Himself for our sins so that we could be saved. If we really want to inherit heaven, let us stop storing up treasures for ourselves here on earth. We are busy nowadays with the developments of the world such as; fashion, models, the posh lifestyle and many other things. It is good to have a good life but do we desire whole heartedly to be with Jesus, the innocent Lamb who died just for you and me so that we can be saved? May the Lord forgive our sins and help us inherit His kingdom. The story reflects realities of our life therefore, we may say a little prayer to God:

Our Heavenly Father, teaches us to love more than anything and reminds us in our daily life that it was His one and only Son who sacrificed himself because of us. In Jesus name I have prayed. Amen.

TODAY GOD IS PASSING WITH HIS GLORY AND BLESSING

God is passing in your life today. Surely, He is! We may have been waiting a long time for Him. It takes time for us to receive answers for our prayers and dreams. May be it takes time for blessings and His mercies to come to us? It might be His glory, it might be His love, it might be His healing, or it might be His power. God gives us what is the best for us and we say God did not answer me while He blesses in other ways like; a health life. So that whatever we dream should be given in health life. In short, we should understand that God's plan is different from ours. Therefore, we should petition to him and wait patiently for his response.

Closely, let us look at the book of Exodus. Now therefore, I pray, if I have found grace in Your sight, show me now Your way, that I may know You and that I may find grace in Your sight. And consider that this nation is Your people." And He said, "My Presence will go with you, and I will give you rest." Then he said to Him, "If Your Presence does not go with us, do not bring us up from here. For how then will it be known that Your people and I have found grace in Your sight, except You go with us? So we shall be separate, Your people and I, from all the people who are upon the face of the earth." So the Lord said to Moses, "I will also do this thing that you have spoken; for you have found grace in My sight, and I know you by name." And he said, "Please, show me Your glory." Then He said, "I will make all My goodness pass before you, and I will proclaim the name of the Lord before you. I will be gracious to whom I will be gracious, and I will have compassion on whom I will have compassion." But He said, "You cannot see My face; for no man shall see Me, and live." And the Lord said, "Here is a place by Me, and you shall stand on the rock. So it shall be, while My glory passes by, that I will put you in the cleft of the rock, and will cover you with My hand while I pass by. Then I will take away My hand, and you shall see My back; but My face shall not be seen." (Exodus 33:13-23 KJV)

We can see how Moses enjoyed the presents and that glory of the Lord. This did not only happen to him but also to Elisha, when Elijah was leaving this world going to our Father in Heaven. And so it was, when they had crossed over, that Elijah said to Elisha, "Ask! What may I do for you, before I am taken away from you?" Elisha said, "Please let a double portion of your spirit be upon me." So he said, you have asked a hard thing. Nevertheless, if you see me when I am taken from you, it shall be so for you; but if not, it shall not be so." (2Kings2:9-10KJV).

Furthermore, when Jesus Christ was going to Heaven the men were looking at Him up in the sky and the two men dressed in white said the way you see him going, the same way will come back to take us one day.

From the three stories which have been highlighted, we can observe that it can be a waste of time not to believe in God. God is real and ask Him what you want and we should be wise to seek His kingdom as the bible tells us that seek first the kingdom of God and His righteousness and all will come to us. Choose God today, let the hearing, richness, worth, and many more be the bonus for us. May be we want to see God now? Then we need to be patient with God and we will see Him. God visits us in so many ways like hearing His voice, Comfort, dreams and many more. He is a mystery God. Have we been suffering? call God now He will listen to you and He will come near you and give you what you are looking for. Ask Him now it might be your chance for you to meet God and tell Him all your needs. God wants us to enjoy His presence as well. If we seek His presence then we will be in His plan.

ARE YOU PART OF GOD'S PLAN?

"And we know that in all things God works for the good of those who love him, who have been called according to his purpose" (Romans 8:28 NIV). Have you ever asked yourself," why all this, Lord, one thing after another? Take this verse and see if it applies to what has been happening in your life. If you are part of God's plan you will see that all your plans will never work, but His plan(s) will work. Sometimes we complain just because we deny the truth. Sometimes we do not have time to ask God about His plan for us. My dear friend, you need to let God's plan to work in our lives now. Someone can ask "God's plan?" "What are you trying to say?"

The story of Abraham answers us. The father of many nations, Abraham was part of God's plan, that is why he left his family members and he followed God. He also let his people and animals die and suffer in the desert. Even the King was cursed by him. He also patiently waited for the Lord to grant him the child. You can see we are all called his children because Abraham is the father of many nations. Imagine if God had given Abraham a chance to see the world today, He would not believe that he is our father since what happens in the world now is chaotic.

Noah was also in God's plan, the lunatic. People said he was mad. How could God let water from the clouds destroy us since they had never seen rain before? They asked Noah such questions a number of times. However, the so called mad man finished the construction of the ark and called all animals on board: all the animals understood and obeyed instead of the people who were supposed to help him build the ark. Although the people did not listen to him he did not drawback for he entered the ark then locked up. His madness saved him and all the animals. Was he really mad? Many people did not understand God's plan hence they viewed Noah as a mad person.

Moses was another part of the God's plan. He was raised in Egyptian for 40 years and went for 40 years to make a family before coming at the age of 80 to boldly tell pharaoh that "he should let the Israelites go." Though Moses had run from Egypt and forgotten, God never forgot in His plan, He still found Moses, who suffered a lot with the Israelites. Moses stood for Israelite in the presence of Pharaoh and told Him that "God has seen the cry of His people hence it is time for God's people to go and have their peace." Even though Pharaoh was not able to let them go because he knew that his city was built by them and he thought he had power to stop the Israelites. But with the help of God the Israelites went out of Egypt with joy and glory of the Lord.

Let us not forget this wise, innocent, young and brave man Joseph. Joseph valued his virginity or holiness than evil deeds. This is a young man who stood by his God hence he had dignity and respect for others. Indeed, A man who did favours to everyone without expecting anything in return. The story of Joseph teaches us to forgive and save our enemies (relative) or anyone who does bad thing in order to harm us. If you want to be the best man, be like Joseph who was grown by the words of the Lord without parental care or brotherly love.

From all these examples I believe we can understand how God's plans work on us. If you are part of God's plan do not expect people to love you. If you are in God's purpose, your own thinking and ambition will not work except His will work. If you are part of God's plan you will always be underneath people's expectation. Many will have pens and bookmark for your life but if you are in God's plan one day you will wake up and you will be on top of such people. Be in God's plan so that you will know why you are the way you are now. Indeed you may look like you are in need but you never be in lack because with Him you are contented and others may admired. Suffice to say that when you are in God's plan others may compete with you. Nevertheless, God and you will have everlasting joy in all season of lives. Thus in joy or pain, winter, spring and summer it will be well.

DO NOT LET GOD'S BLESSING PASS YOU TODAY

2KINGS 2:10 "You have asked a difficult thing," Elijah said, "yet if you see me when I am taken from you, it will be yours—otherwise, it will not" (NIV). Let us remember that when Elijah was going to heaven, he asked Elisha what he wanted because Elisha was not letting him go. So Elisha said he wanted the double portion of his power. Then Elijah said you have asked a difficult thing because he knew that his power came from the Lord alone and he said "see me when I am taken from you otherwise you will not have it." What lessons are we learning today, focus, waiting, faith, realistic and stand firm. Most of the times we miss God's blessings because of our own thinking, losing hope, lack of patience, running against time and competition. There are some things I want us to learn from this man, Elisha the man who was real with his life, he knew what he wanted and he had faith in all things he did. Just imagine Elijah was going to heaven that meant Elisha was not aware of the exact time when Elijah would depart. Furthermore, Elisha did not know the place where Elijah's journey would take place. Although it was like that Elisha was still following Elijah and some people were asking and laughing at him. But he never lost hope because he knew what he was looking for.

Beloved, open your mind and your eyes as well, we all say these words "when God want to bless He never ask anybody." But we are the same people who want God to bless us in the same way and we are the same people with full of competition and we fail to wait for the Lord. We always find the backup plan. Let me tell you that short cut is always long. The other problem is that we are not real when we go in the presences of the Lord. We need a favour from Him while on the other side we are busy with the world hence we are dishonest. We miss God because we do not want Him, we want to use Him. How can you use your creator the owner of all things we see and cannot see? Most of the times we lie to God that if he does something to us then we will do this and that to others, but after wards we forget what we said. God never lie and we cannot cheat Him. Be real when we are in God's presence, focus on the Lord alone, never look at people, do not allow yourself to lose His blessings because you are expecting what He has done to others, book your own order from the Lord. We are unique as evident through our skin, wisdom, food we eat, whether that suits us, lifestyle and we are all good in the eyes of the Lord our God. God will bless us when we ask Him and wait patiently.

GOD'S BLESSING AMONG US

GENESIS 45:9 Hurry and go up to my father, and say to him, thus says your son Joseph: "God has made me lord of all Egypt; come down to me, do not tarry" (KJV). I just want us to see how God's blessing work to us, it was Joseph whom God blessed and as we can remember Joseph was forgotten in his family. The father knew that he was dead and the brothers knew that he was taken into slavery, to them Joseph was gone and what remained was only history of him. But when God blessed him, he did not see himself as someone else or boost to his relatives "that look at me now, who is the loser now?" But he humbled himself and took them back and even took all his people to Egypt. What do we do when God blesses us? Leave our family members aside and have our own life, forget about them? We have to learn from Joseph that what God gives us we need to share. In other words, when God blesses, He blesses you He even blesses your family members. May be you are a man of God and God works in you and many people are reaching God and their needs through you and you have many problems in your life never give up. God's time is the best just know that we shall overcome as time goes by. Remind God today that when you are going to bless me do not forget my family members as you did to Joseph, David, Abraham, Joshua, Daniel, Jacob, Moses, Noah family, Lot and the girls and many more in the bible. God promises us to bless us from generation to generation. We have to claim our blessing to God today Claim your blessings today.

CHAPTER TWO

In God We Trust

Have you ever been in a confused situation state? Even your money can not buy it, even parent and any relationship cannot help? This is the time you need God and God alone. Think of a woman who is delivering would she allow her new born baby dying during her delivery? She cannot allow her dream of seeing her fruits of her womb not reviewed. There are many difficult situations in life that sometimes we cannot forward them or skip them. In that trial of life never waste time to use your wisdom like committing suicide, witchdoctors or witchcraft, or show the world how desperate you are. God allow us to pass through that way so that we can understand Him. For instance; Joseph was betrayed by his relatives because of the strange dreams he had, the dream was not filled yet and it take years for it to be done. But they choose to betray their young brother and threw him in the pit. As Joseph was punished with the dream he had, it's a lesson to us to avoid telling anyone things that appear to us in a vision because the Devil is everywhere even in our relatives. What was he thinking in the cistern? Indeed, if you were put in the pit and you were thrown there with the clothes? What would be your next plan? Perhaps you would give up; such is life or cry to God for help. In such situations we need God and God alone not anyone. Other ways are just wrong ways, if you want to make your way easy the only answer is God. God has order in all his ways so if you are too fast, you will end up being late. Let His order and time work on us. Sometimes, I wonder particularly, when I feel tired of waiting for God's help. I often say God you created everything in six days and you rested on the seventh day as well, how come now you are failing to work on me as days are passing and years are going by too? However, there is a simple answer God firstly created a place for us, made a good living for us He gave us everything that we might need then He created us. This means that when God is working on us He wants us to have content and to appreciate His good work. God is the master planner of our life and He always keep His words to us, He never lies. Wait for his time and do His will. God takes time to give us so that we can understand His goodness and know how to use it. He always wants us to remember Him alone and never to be boastful by praising our capabilities. For instance; because of my education that is why I am where I am, because of my wisdom that is why I am here, because of money that is why I have a heath life. Generally, you see all that I have, its because of my money. Let God be God in our life. Jeremiah 18; 6 "O house of Israel, cannot I do with you as this potter? saith the LORD. Behold, as the clay is in the potter's hand, so are ye in mine hand, O house of Israel (KJV). Yes we are in His hands let us patiently wait for Him for He is above everything.

SOMEBODY TOUCH ME

Jesus asked who touched him. It is the story we used to hear or read time to time. But I want us today to hear it in another way. Mark 5:24-34 "24 So Jesus went with him. A large crowd followed and pressed around him. 25 And a woman was there who had been subject to bleeding for twelve years. 26 She had suffered a great deal under the care of many doctors and had spent all she had, yet instead of getting better she grew worse. 27 When she heard about Jesus, she came up behind him in the crowd and touched his cloak, 28 because she thought, "If I just touch his clothes, I will be healed." 29 Immediately her bleeding stopped and she felt in her body that she was freed from her suffering. [30]

At once Jesus realized that power had gone out of him. He turned around in the crowd and asked, "Who touched my clothes?" [31]

"You see the people crowding against you," his disciples answered, "and yet you can ask,'

Who touched me?' " [32] But Jesus kept looking around to see who had done it. [33] Then the woman, knowing what had happened to her, came and fell at his feet and, trembling with fear, told him the whole truth. [34] He said to her, "Daughter, your faith has healed you. Go in peace and be freed from your suffering,"(NIV). Are we tired with our trials? This woman was sick and she spent everything she had to get better but things got worse, she suffered: bleeding for twelve years. Nevertheless, she never lost hope and she believed that one day she shall be fine.

Look at yourself do you still have hope that one day you will be fine? Is it cancer because many have been dead of it and it means that you cannot be healed? Is it AIDS that makes you feel like you are already dead? What is it? Whatever it is have faith, you shall overcome it someday. The woman heard about Jesus and she went there and as a woman it was hard to explain her problem in front of everybody. And the second reason was that the woman she looked to Jesus as His son. Hence she thought: "How can I tell Him about my problems at the same time of meeting?" However she thought; "the way I heard stories about Him let me touch His clothes and I will be healed." Then she decided to do what she thought and on the sport the bleeding stopped and she was healed. For how long are you going to cry for the same problem while we know that what we believe in has failed us and there is no other way? Try Jesus today with faith touch His clothes, it does not need others to know, it needs how humble, innocent and faith you have for Him to make things alright. Jesus realised that His power had gone out, and He knew that somebody had used his power with her faith so as to get healed and she became normal again.

When He asked, others tried to shut Him up, Yes! We have such people in our life they always want to silence people in life and they will always make us wrong. Although we will have them in our life, at the same time things will be alright to us. Let them live the way they do while God controls our things. Sometimes we are found in places which are busy, noisy and many activities but if we touch Jesus something will change, we will have what we want and what we are looking for the long time. Do not wait for the perfect time and place for God to intervene in your life. Remember, He never sleeps and He is always there for us. Talk to Him today if you want to get better, talk to Him if you want things to change in your life. The woman came up to introduce herself to Jesus and to the crowd that she was the one who touched him. And she even said what she was thinking before touching Him. Then Jesus said "your faith has healed you." We need to be like her, we should do things with faith, let others hear the history of it. Let us go in the presence of the Lord with faith and we will come up with what we want. Let our suffering be a story to others who named us the suffering itself. Let it be history to our life first which will be a blessing to us. We need to have a new story in our life starting from today. May the good Lord bless His words today and let it flow like a river in our hearts and reach each and every place.

TRUST IN THE LORD

John 14: Let not your heart be troubled: ye believe in God, believe also in me (KJV). What can we learn today from this simple verse? The verse that is in our hearts; we can say anytime. I want us today to go deeper with this verse. It says do not let your heart be "troubled", that means there are many ways our hearts can be troubled. Doubt is fear, searching for many ways is fear, looking for attention is fear, looking for a shoulder to cry on is fear. In other words, if we have God and trust in Him we have no fear we have faith that our God will do everything and is always there. And if we have God all things I write on top is just a story because we know that our God is beyond that. When you go to the doctor to get tested, what do you expect from the doctor? Most of the times we are filled with fear regarding our results as to what in will they be positive or negative. We tend to think; may be it is cancer, may be my condition is worse. What we have is fear? Take note if you have trust in your friend or people, you end up being controlled when you lose confidence in yourself. Thus; you will fail to handle yourself, your family, even have no time for your God. If you put your trust in anything you believe than God, you are a person who will never have peace and joy of the Lord. Why am I saying so? Your life will end up being in a competition, challenge, lack of peace, looking for others to praise you, always want to be like others, and want to try everything. In a nutshell your life will be in the opposite of the above verse. Trust in the Lord, no matter what? Even when all people you love and close to run away from you, your life will be the same and God will guide you in all times and He will be with you always. Where are your pride, porch life and boots? Put your pride in the Lord and you never suffer lack. If you have pride in the Lord you will do it, even hundreds of people say wait for him and he will fail soon. They are the ones who will fall before you and because God is love you will be the one pulling them up and even help and support them. My God is God who exalts beyond our expectation and if we trust in him, indeed, we will see his mercies, love, favour, peace, comfort, help and kindness. Remember He has thousands ways to take a good care of us. And before we were born and before everything we see or we did not see our God was there. And He knows the best and any place we are, we were there because of His plans. Not the plan of our family, our parents, our husbands, our wife, our children, our work and the money. It's because of Him and God alone not anyone.

CHAPTER THREE

Part One: Health with God

Which food did God give us to eat?

Why we are not supposed to eat the other?

Leviticus 11 (NIV)

Clean and Unclean Food

"1 The Lord said to Moses and Aaron, 2 Say to the Israelites: Of all the animals that live on land, these are the ones you may eat: 3 You may eat any animal that has a divided hoof and that chews the cud. 4 There are some that only chew the cud or only have a divided hoof, but you must not eat them. The camel, though it chews the cud, does not have a divided hoof; it is ceremonially unclean for you. 5 The hyrax, though it chews the cud, does not have a divided hoof; it is unclean for you. 6 The rabbit, though it chews the cud, does not have a divided hoof; it is unclean for you. 7 And the pig, though it has a divided hoof, does not chew the cud; it is unclean for you. 8 You must not eat their meat or touch their carcasses; they are unclean for you. 9 of all the creatures living in the water of the seas and the streams you may eat any that have fins and scales. 10 But all creatures in the seas or streams that do not have fins and scales—whether among all the swimming things or among all the other living creatures in the water—you are to regard as unclean. 11 And since you are to regard them as unclean, you must not eat their meat; you must regard their carcasses as unclean. 12 Anything living in the water that does not have fins and scales is to be regarded as unclean by you. 13 These are the birds you are to regard as unclean and not eat because they are unclean: the eagle, the vulture, the black vulture, 14 the red kite, any kind of black kite, 15 any kind of raven, 16 the horned owl, the screech owl, the gull, any kind of hawk, 17 the little owl, the cormorant, the great owl, 18 the white owl, the desert owl, the osprey, 19 the stork, any kind of heron, the hoopoe and the bat. 20 All flying insects that walk on all fours are to be regarded as unclean by you. 21 There are, however, some flying insects that walk on all fours that you may eat: those that have jointed legs for hopping on the ground. 22 Of these you may eat any kind of locust, katydid, cricket or grasshopper. 23 But all other flying insects that have four legs you are to regard as unclean. 24 You will make yourselves unclean by these; whoever touches their carcasses will be unclean till evening. 25 Whoever picks up one of their carcasses must wash their clothes, and they will be unclean till evening. 26 Every animal that does not have a divided hoof or that does not chew the cud is unclean for you; whoever touches the carcass of any of them will be unclean. 27 Of all the animals that walk on all fours, those that walk on their paws are unclean for you; whoever touches their carcasses will be unclean till evening. 28 Anyone who picks up their carcasses must wash their clothes, and they will be unclean till evening. These animals are unclean for you. 29 Of the animals that move along the ground, these are unclean for you: the weasel, the rat, any kind of great lizard, 30 the gecko, the monitor lizard, the wall lizard, the skink and the chameleon. 31 Of all those that move along the ground, these are unclean for you. Whoever touches them when they are dead will be unclean till evening. 32 When one of them dies and falls on something, that article, whatever its use, will be unclean, whether it is made of wood, cloth, hide or sackcloth. Put it in water; it will be unclean till evening, and then it will be clean. 33 If one of them falls into a clay pot, everything in it will be unclean, and you must break the pot. 34 Any food you are allowed to eat that has come into contact with water from any such pot is unclean, and any liquid that is drunk from such a pot is unclean. 35 Anything that one of their carcasses falls on becomes unclean; an oven or cooking pot must be broken up. They are unclean, and you are to regard them as unclean. 36 A spring, however, or a cistern for collecting water remains clean, but anyone who touches one of these carcasses is unclean. 37 If a carcass falls on any seeds that are to be planted, they remain clean. 38 But if water has been put on the seed and a carcass falls on it, it is unclean for you. 39 If an animal that you are allowed to eat dies, anyone who touches its carcass will be unclean till evening. 40 Anyone who eats some of its carcass must wash their clothes, and they will be unclean till evening. Anyone who picks up the carcass must wash their clothes, and they will be unclean till evening. 41 Every creature that moves along the ground is to be regarded as unclean; it is not to be eaten. 42 You are not to eat any creature that moves along the ground, whether it moves on its belly or walks on all fours or on many feet; it is unclear. 43 Do not defile yourselves by any of these creatures. Do not make yourselves unclean by means of them or be made unclean by them. 44 I am the Lord your God; consecrate yourselves and be holy, because I am holy. Do not make yourselves unclean by any creature that moves along the ground. 45 I am the Lord, who brought you up out of Egypt to be your God; therefore be holy, because I am holy. 46 These are the regulations concerning animals, birds, every living thing that moves about in the water and every creature that moves along the ground. 47 You must distinguish between the unclean and the clean, between living creatures that may be eaten and those that may not be eaten" (NIV).

Part Two: Health with God

We have seen that in Leviticus 11 God tells us what we are supposed to Eat. Why did God give us food? Genesis 1:29-30 "Then God said," I give you every seed-bearing plant on the face of the whole earth and every tree that has fruit with seed in it. They will be yours for food. And to all beast of the earth and all the birds of the air and all creatures that has the breath of life in it-I give every green plant for food. And it was so" (NIV). Wow! Initially God gave us plants to eat. Why did God give us plants to eat not meat? He gave us plants because plants work best in our bodies, plants control systems of the body, like digestion, fat, level of sugar, water and more nutrients we find in plants. Plants are also medicine in our body. Eating of meat has resulted into fighting for diet, cancer and so may diseases.

Then why did things change to start eating animals? Indeed, why did God give us type of animals we are supposed to eat and some which not to? Things changed when flood came in and covered the earth. After the flood the earth was full of water and the plants were being destroyed so God told Noah to eat animals as well. Genesis 9:3 "Everything that lives and moves will be food for you. Just as I gave you the green plants, I now give you everything" (NIV). We can see now how things changed for us. God wanted us to be vegetarians because most of plants are medicine to our body. But after the flood He himself found food for us, on Leviticus 11 He gave us what we are supposed to eat. Because God is the maker and he knows best how much our bodies need and what is importance for our body to function well. And why did He say we shall not eat blood and fat? God warned us not to eat fat because it's not good for our healthy. This is also evident today as doctors advise us not to eat more Jacky foods because they have a lot of fats which are harmful to our bodies. More diseases nowadays are due to fats for instance; high blood pressure comes because of the blocking of veins in the body stroke, obesity starts because of cholesterol. That means God knows much more of our body than our self He also says your body is the temple of the Lord. Because our body is the temple, we should be careful of what we are feeding. He also says you shall not eat blood, He says in blood there is life so by eating animals it means we grasp such life of animals we partake. This entails that other habits we have are because of the blood we eat from other food. Most food we are taking now becomes problem to our bodies. We must take care of what we consume. If we need to eat meat let us eat only what God gave us on Leviticus and mind you when taking it make sure we are not taking the fats and the blood. Most diseases are result of disobedient because God already warned us. Let us follow God's instruction and live healthy and peaceful life. We have a lot of work in this world to do, to spread the word of our Father in Heaven, Jesus choose us to do that work. How could we do it if we are sick? Please let us help each other to live healthy.

I KNEW YOU BEFORE YOU WERE IN YOUR MOTHERS WOMB

Jeremiah 1:5 Before I formed thee in the belly I knew thee; and before thou camest forth out of the womb I sanctified thee and I ordained thee a prophet unto the nations" (JKV). Now my questions are: why do we say we are not ready when you are pregnant or you impregnate? Why do we abort babies? Why do we run away from responsibilities? Why do we flash, kill, and run away from our babies? God tells us here in Jeremiah 1: 5 He knew us before we were formed in the womb, why do we take God's part and use it as back up by killing innocent babies. Doctors, Men and all who support this idea of killing babies, why don't you use same Idea to bring back life from someone who has died today, your relative, your loved ones? God says He set us apart, means He has a good plan for us why don't we give a chance to those innocent babies? May be we are killing people who would have changed the world? God assigned us many duties of this world, when we kill those innocent babies have we ever asked ourselves why do our parents give us this precious gift of life? Let us have children by the choice of the Lord not by choice of ourselves. We might be clever to have children by the choice of ours but we might not have the capacity to raise them. Ladies how do you feel to raise a child, while we have killed another innocent gift from God? How sure are we that this baby is perfect than the other we chose to kill?

TILL DEATH DO US PART

We used to say this on the wedding day as wedding blessings. Now I want to tell you to think about the same words but in a negative way, are the words good to make it a promise to the lovers?

Why am I saying this?

Yes till death do us part, the devil uses the same words to attack us? Sometimes we choose death to do other part. What do you think when you are cheating your partner? Clearly, you are killing the happiness so that death can do your marriage to part. Death is not only cheating, it can mean many things such as In-law when they control too much. If the two people choose to be together that means they depend on each other why should in-laws part them? When you part them it means your death. But why do we choose to be thorns in a fresh or be happy to be destroyers? Some ladies you are death as well, you are happy when a man comes to you and states the weakness of his wife and "you are busy saying He loves me I will give him everything." But who are you to be death. All of you who are involved in ending other people's marriage and happiness just know that you are death in the fresh of happiness. There are evil people again when the see a problem in their marriage they say "well I cannot do divorce you know what divorce is very shameful thing." Instead I will simple kill my wife or my husband, so that I can inherit the property, remarry again then have my kids and I will be free from all the abuse. We are busy plotting and finding solution(s) in the name of death. We are busy drugging them, causing problems like diseases, putting poison on their cosmetics and food. Finding unnecessary problems to pull down but who are you to be death? God clearly tells us thou shall not kill. Why killing joy, happiness, innocent people, and blessed marriages? If we are involved in such situations we better seek forgiveness to God. Let me tell you this if you ever acted like this to somebody just know that you are dead person in God's eyes. Colossians 2:13 "And you, being dead in your sins and the uncircumcision of your flesh, hath he quickened together with him, having forgiven you all trespasses" (KJV). Sometimes we lie to ourselves that it's fine because I did not feel guilty of it. Certainly, we are a dead person that is why we do not have any conscious. We need to seek God's holy spirits to guide us, so that we can be living people again.

WHY ARE WE DYING?

There was a family where the father was unfaithful, that man was having an affair. When the woman found out she forgave the man but the man was insulting the wife, comparing her with the affair woman. The woman was very depressed about it and she was not a quitter, she could always fight for what she loved and she made a big mistake trying to be like the woman who was cheating with her husband. But when the husband observed that, he knew that the woman will not let him go. In a way the wife did not accept the weakness of the husband. The husband continued ignoring her hence she was very angry and killed her own husband. Sometimes we have to be careful with our action(s) that is why we need God in our lives. Some situations are beyond our control to handle them with our thoughts. Let us see the same story in the bible, how Uriah 2Samuel 11:5-24 the woman conceived and sent word to David, saying, "I am pregnant." 6 So David sent this word to Joab: "Send me Uriah the Hittite." And Joab sent him to David. 7 When Uriah came to him, David asked him how Joab was, how the soldiers were and how the war was going. 8 Then David said to Uriah, "Go down to your house and wash your feet." So Uriah left the palace, and a gift from the king was sent after him. 9 But Uriah slept at the entrance to the palace with all his master's servants and did not go down to his house. 10 David was told, "Uriah did not go home." So he asked Uriah, "Haven't you just come from a military campaign? Why didn't you go home?" 11 Uriah said to David, "The ark and Israel and Judah are staying in tents and my commander Joab and my Lord's men are camped in the open country. How could I go to my house to eat and drink and make love to my wife? As surely as you live, I will not do such a thing!" 12 Then David said to him, "Stay here one more day, and tomorrow I will send you back." So Uriah remained in Jerusalem that day and the next. 13 At David's invitation, he ate and drank with him and David made him drunk. But in the evening Uriah went out to sleep on his mat among his master's servants; he did not go home. 14 In the morning David wrote a letter to Joab and sent it with Uriah. 15 In it he wrote: "Put Uriah out in front where the fighting is fiercest. Then withdraw from him so he will be struck down and die." 16 So while Joab had the city under siege, he put Uriah at a place where he knew the strongest defenders were. 17 When the men of the city came out and fought against Joab, some of the men in David's army fell; moreover, Uriah the Hittite died. 18 Joab sent David a full account of the battle. 19 He instructed the messenger: "When you have finished giving the king this account of the battle, 20 the king's anger may flare up, and he may ask you, "Why did you get so close to the city to fight?" Didn't you know they would shoot arrows from the wall? 21 Who killed Abimelek son of Jerub-Besheth[b]? Didn't a woman drop an upper millstone on him from the wall, so that he died in Thebez "Why did you get so close to the wall?" If he asks you this, then say to him, "moreover, your servant Uriah the Hittite is dead." 22 The messenger set out, and when he arrived he told David everything Joab had sent him to say. 23 The messenger said to David, "The men overpowered us and came out against us in the open, but we drove them back to the entrance of the city gate. 24 Then the archers shot arrows at your servants from the wall and some of the king's men died. Moreover, your servant Uriah the Hittite is dead" (NIV). We can see how Uriah died innocently and he never allowed getting involved in covering up somebody's mess. Do we trust and fear God in all things we have. Uriah trusted God and believed to put innocence in the hands of God. It's good to trust the Lord even if you die, the truth shall be reviewed one day than to cover up and be broken. Many people nowadays choose to be involved in other's mess as the story we saw earlier own, whereby the woman was innocent but her action made her to serve in hell. We need to involve God, if we have God, He will Judge for us and He is the only one who see all secret things. Above all, He will never let us suffer with the devil's abuses. Even when we think we can handle anything on our own, we are always wrong. We must always remember that we are nothing but pencils in the hands of the Creator.

WHAT IS FAMILY

A family starts between a woman and a man. These people make a commitment between themselves to live together not as friends but lovers. Family starts with friendship; the talk, the laughter, communication through signs and signals. They are soul mates not because they march in the appearance but they are connected in the soul and the body. If you are in love with your lover you need to speak the same language, when you are talking they need to be like I was about to say the same word. Lovers need to miss each other hence they would be saying "I was thinking about you and I was about to call, thank you call first." The first degree of marriage is communication. For example; if you believe that when I call my friend elsewhere, I will have answers then what about with your partner? In family there is a need for a bond, where the married couple has to mate. Love making God gave us as a gift that we need to relax in the mind, exercise, feeling special and make a bond. And if we are lucky in love making we have a gift of children. After paying the bills, tough day, stressed, missing each other we need to make love to refresh ourselves. There is a secret in love making because your blood mixed together. If you are naked and she or he is naked and join in that way there is a secret. That is why when there is any suspicious act you ask if everything is ok. If are cheating, your partner can know without hear from somewhere, and all the strange emotions can be known easily because you are connected. As such we need to be very careful to what we do with our partner sometimes, if it is perfect couple you look alike or look good when you are together.

Family is a secret, what happens inside nobody knows except the ones in it, even kids live in that family parent's life style. Sometimes kids say if you ask dad he will give you the same answer mum answered. And kids know us better than we think, if you are fighting they will know through your answers. And they are the ones who suffer because they are visitors in a family. We shall not destroy the innocent souls because of our childish. Cheating has no back up (an excuse), you are the one you choose that lady or man to marry. Thus; you made a choice to live with her or him. Therefore marry someone because of who they are not because of what they have. It is the case since when the latter is not available then marriage will not be there too. Cheating is selfish; lack of confident, challenge, childish, in short it's evil. If you think that your partner is worse he cannot change, then understand. But if it is a habit do not worry because every habit can change with time. You cheat because you never have time to know the best in her or him; you cheat because you never have a time to learn about her or him and you are worse than her or him that is why you are looking for a way out. Somebody to cry to or beg for love it does not show or mean to you that you are important. This simply shows how weak you are since you always seek attention to prove that you love or you are important.

Strong men or women never cheat they find a way to go ahead or to live with their partner. If you do not like her or him why don't you let her live instead of cheating. You go out there because you are the one who fear: "who is going to love me again; I should be the first one to find someone." If she or he is not good in bed whose fault is that, teach him or her you need to be open to your partner than going out with some people. Find time for him or her. If she is not looking good whose fault is that? You are lazy for you do not have time to look and buy her what you want her to have. Ladies make your man be the man you dream him to be. If she is housewife give her something to make her busy since at home its tiresome talking with kids all day long. Find a nanny for her to give her break, have special time together; have a tour, have a good time together and talk like adults make future together. Make a lot of laughter(s) together less fight, fight reasonable to build up.

When you have more income than men learn to build your men, show him how much you adore him money without money it's okay. I do not know what you do in your family but at least do not have boundaries. You need to know the income you are having and make budget together through that way you will find that you will have more money to spend or to keep it for other things. Do not use your car to carry prostitute(s) instead of your wife and the kids. If the other partner is not working, you need to include him or her in your money let her or him be the accountant of the home do not let her or him be the child or the maid in her own house because one day she or he will fight for own freedom. Do not build a curtain, let him or her have your password, passport number, touch your phone and have your account number. Do not put a boundary in your lovely family and trust in each other more than anybody. You will see even people outside will not interfere with your family affairs. All thorns in your family burn them and start together again. If you stop fighting one other you will be happy no matter what. Because you will support each other in anything even in-laws will never come across you. Let the in-laws talk about you together, protect your partner. Let others say outside if the wife gave you that answer the husband will answer you the same. Do not let others separate you because of your weakness, let them build you up.

Remember if we want our wife to obey us, we need to love her. These two work together likewise, if we want our husband to love us we need to respect him. Stop respecting other men than your man. Give your man power then he will love you. Learn to miss each other. And learn to talk positively to your partner even in public places. Do not leave the most precious thing that God gave you because of lack of time to learn about it. Living together means understanding one another and that is what God wants us to be.

CHAPTER FOUR

Word

JOHN 1; 1 in the beginning was the Word and the Word was with God and the Word was God (JKV). Let's remind each other that God's creation was done through His word and He simply said "let there be," for instance; let there be light and the light was formed. God used His words to create all things we see and we did not see. It was His words which created everything, except we human beings He said let's make a man and He made us from the dust and His on breathe. Today, we are dealing with words, God created through words. God speaks through words and His words will remain for ever. And he warned us not to add or subtract His words, and He also said "I will put my words into you." His words are so powerful. His words teach us, discipline us, give us hope, promise us, make us feel His presence and save us. God breathe on us and He made us in His own image hence we have also power in words. We can see the world is full of speeches, books, talks, and communication hence we need to be very careful with words. Our words create, curse and also bless. In this year, let's try to talk positive to ourselves and to our friends as well. Stop talking in a negative way, start believing in yourself and admire. You know what? If we start doing things in a positive way and to our friends, we will achieve a lot this year. Stop looking for the weakness in others. We should stop saying like; my words are powerful you cannot do this to me you shall see. Who are you? Why being happy when somebody is in problems. Hatred is a wasting of time, stop handling things in your own, leave it to God He is a good judge.

WISDOM COMES FROM THE LORD

(1 CORINTHIANS 3:18-19) 18 Let no man deceive himself. If any man among you seemeth to be wise in this world, let him become a fool, that he may be wise. [19] For the wisdom of this world is foolishness with God. For it is written, He taketh the wise in their own craftiness (KJV). These two verses tell us how foolish we are when we believe in our wisdom. And the verses show us that all wisdom we use by our age and craftiness are from the deception of the devil. The world is full of sinful nature because we choose to have our own wisdom. Why do we have sex change, homosexual, Unfaithful, killing, extreme scientific ideas, economy problems, strikes, drugs? With our wisdom same things we make harm us in turn. For example; we make condoms to prevent Aids and pregnancy, look now the percentage of aids is increasing and many marriages are destroyed because of lack of faithfulness. We make guns for protection, now the world is a victim of wars and death. Let us use God's wisdom in our lives for the good peace and joyful life again. God cries for us today for all those painful moments we are passing through. God is quiet aware that we found ourselves in such situations because we hate God's wisdom and control.

WHO IS YOUR FRIEND

Friends are people who have developed a mutual understanding together. A friend is a person who always be there for you during good times and even when things turn to mess. I have experienced earthly friendship when things turn into sour they scattered and show their pair of hooves as if a dog is chasing them. JOHN 15: 14. "Ye are my friends if you do whatsoever I command you Jesus" Anyone can be a true friend of Jesus if we are devoted Christians and as long as we follow Memorandum of understanding. Furthermore, we can be His friend if we do whatever He commands us to do. Christ here is giving us unconditional friendship. This love is going to every one rich or poor, married or unmarried, young or Old. Make a Date with Christ.

PRAYER

Prayer is a powerful device; it connects us with Our Father and makes our journey easy on this earth. Jesus teaches us to call the kingdom of God as it is in heaven it has to came on earth as well, He also wants us to have food to eat and He says we should ask God for daily bread both spiritual and body. And when you pray, do not be like the hypocrites, for they love to pray standing in the synagogues and on the street corners to be seen by others. Truly I tell you, they have received their reward in full. We are on how to pray in Matthew 6:6-15 But thou, when thou prayest, enter into thy closet, and when thou hast shut thy door, pray to thy Father which is in secret; and thy Father which seeth in secret shall reward thee openly. But when ye pray, use not vain repetitions, as the heathen do: for they think that they shall be heard for their much speaking.Be not ye therefore like unto them: for your Father knoweth what things ye have need of, before ye ask him. After this manner therefore pray ye: Our Father which art in heaven, Hallowed be thy name. Thy kingdom come, Thy will be done in earth, as it is in heaven. Give us this day our daily bread. And forgive us our debts, as we forgive our debtors. And lead us not into temptation, but deliver us from evil: For thine is the kingdom, and the power, and the glory, for ever. Amen. For if ye forgive men their trespasses, your heavenly Father will also forgive you: But if ye forgive not men their trespasses, neither will your Father forgive your trespasses (NIV).

CHAPTER FIVE

Why the Devil Hides His Identity

The devil fears the Lord our God, because of this fear he uses anything against God even human beings. He hides because He knows how great our God is. Firstly, he used a snake to win over human beings. And his mission worked. He makes us suffer up to an extent that we say there is no God hence we idolatry worshipping other gods than God in heaven. Or being disobedient to the word of God and live carelessly forgetting that this world is not our home.

The Devil confuses people with lies that we can control ourselves without any power of God, we can control earth it's our land and we are wise enough to control everything. But is it true that we are controlling the earth? Obviously, the answer is no. Devil hides his identity and makes a lot of kingship while he is busy controlling us in the name of our fellow human beings. In a way the devil wears a mask. This is evident in the bible, precisely, in Matthew16; 23 "Jesus said to peter, "Get behind me, Satan! You are a stumbling-block to me; you do not have in mind the things of God, but the things of men" (NIV). We can see here that Satan was busy blocking Jesus to speak and Jesus was very tired with him and He just told him that he was not righteous like him. This is shows that the devil uses people hence he makes people to sin. But Christ still died for us so that we should be still wearing the helmet of truth and being in His image. Satan wants us to die with him because he knows that God has judged him already and he does not want to die alone, he is a loser and because of that he deceives people. No wonder, he gives us his ideas so that we can blame God for no reason. He does not want us to see God's power on us, you can remember he put Job in trouble and he hacked Daniel prayers. Whether we like it or not, devil is against the people of God. Why is he against us? He knows how great and powerful our Father in Heaven is and he knows that God is with us, He protects us, He never lie and He fulfils His promises amongst us. While the devil is a liar and he runs away and just fools us, kills and destroys us. For this the choice is in our hands, to live or to die.

HIDE AND SEEK

John 8:32 "And ye shall know the truth, and the truth shall make you free" (KJV). This issue is very important to our lives; we have many issues that we do not want to disclose our loved one, like family, friends, relatives, relationships. Indeed, we cannot say them, they are shameful and we do not want to lose our relationships because of such issues. If the world is like this today it's because of hide and seek. We are good in hiding things and make it a secret. Fine it works but do you feel comfortable living someone without knowing anything? The verse above clearly says when you know the truth and tell the truth that's when you are free. We are happy to keep our loved ones in dark because we want them in our lives. Why don't we keep them in free and light so that they have to make a choice in our lives by themselves? Hiding things is fear, fear comes from sin, and sin makes us to feel ashamed. There is a word which says a small scratch makes a wound. Keeping the secret makes the mistake to grow older than we think.

Let us make others love us the way we are and help us to clean our mess than to create secret flight.

THE DEVIL HAS NO PLAN

Job 1:7 "And the LORD said unto Satan, Whence comest thou? Then Satan answered the LORD, and said; from going to and fro in the earth, and from walking up and down in it," (KJV). There was a woman who was a prostitute and that day she went to work as usual. She stood at the road as usual that night and when a car was about to pass by, she stopped it. A man was driving that car and he asked her where she was going and in her sexy and arouse way she responded; "where you are going sir." The man said "well then let's go." The lift was offered. Bear in mind that this woman was a prostitute and she was dressed her good way a night stand. The man drove to his home and the woman was excited. She thought "wow! I will take this man up to the point of taking me to his home? This will be my last day to stand on the road because this man is kind and in his kindness she will make the man to be her forever. If she had known she would not have dreamed of that. When they reached home she was surprised to see the wife and the kids welcoming Dad and the man simply said "honey I brought a visitor she said she was coming here so welcome her I have to refresh myself." The prostitute was very ashamed and she just said I have to leave. Guess what? There were dogs at that home and she slept on the drain. She did not make money and worked on that day, she had a bad day. The story clearly shows that this woman got into trouble because of how she answered "I am going where you are going." We see in Job 1:7 "that the devil is going to and from in the earth and from walking up and down." To work up in the morning and just live without a plan is like giving the devil a loophole to find you. Surely, that is his job moving and searching left, right and centre to find you who have no plan in your life. Indeed, the devil has no plan hence he is searching for us. The devil has no time to say forgive me

Lord because he is waiting for his punishment. Devil is serving his life in prison. And if you have ever been in prison or have an idea of how people stay in prison you would agree with me that death sentence or life in prison is life without hope. How could we allow someone who is serving his sentence to be ruling our lives? Arise! Arise people devil wants to role and destroy our hope, love, faith and even the bond that is there between us and God. Bear in mind this waiting for the time to end and be punished there is no hope, there is waiting only. We need to wait with hope and faith, such waiting gives us courage, strength and believe in all plans of God to us.

THE ORIGIN OF SIN

Rev 12:7-14. [7] And there was war in heaven: Michael and his angels fought against the dragon; and the dragon fought and his angels, [8] And prevailed not; neither was their place found any more in heaven. [9] And the great dragon was cast out, that old serpent, called the Devil, and Satan, which deceiveth the whole world: he was cast out into the earth, and his angels were cast out with him. [10] And I heard a loud voice saying in heaven, Now is come salvation, and strength, and the kingdom of our God, and the power of his Christ: for the accuser of our brethren is cast down, which accused them before our God day and night. [11] And they overcame him by the blood of the Lamb, and by the word of their testimony; and they loved not their lives unto the death. [12] Therefore rejoice, ye heavens, and ye that dwell in them. Woe to the inhabitants of the earth and of the sea! for the devil is come down unto you, having great wrath, because he knoweth that he hath but a short time. [13] And when the dragon saw that he was cast unto the earth, he persecuted the woman which brought forth the man child. [14] And to the woman were given two wings of a great eagle, that she might fly into the wilderness, into her place, where she is nourished for a time, and times, and half a time, from the face of the serpent. (KJV). We can see from the two verses where sin came from. Sin started because of jealous, pride, boastful and competition. God knows what was in the heart of Satan and you know he was the head of the angels and he worked hand in hand with God. Before they waged war with him, God warned Satan, thus; God gave Satan time to change but he was busy planning and deceiving other angels. God saw that Satan would never change and because of that God threw him down from heaven to earth. He chased them from heaven. It is imperative to know the characters of Satan and his biography Ezekiel 28:12-19 [12] Son of man, take up a lamentation for the king of Tyre, and say to him, 'Thus says the Lord GOD: YOU WERE THE SEAL OF PERFECTION, Full of wisdom and perfect in beauty. [13] You were in Eden, the garden of God; every precious stone was your covering: The sardius, topaz, and diamond, Beryl, onyx, and jasper, Sapphire, turquoise, and emerald with gold. The workmanship of your timbrels and pipes were prepared for you on the day you were created. [14] You were the anointed cherub who covers; I established you. You were on the holy mountain of God; You walked back and forth in the midst of fiery stones. [15] You were perfect in your ways from the day you were created, till iniquity was found in you. [16] By the abundance of your trading you became filled with violence within, and you sinned; Therefore, I cast you as a profane thing Out of the mountain of God; And I destroyed you, O covering cherub, from the midst of the fiery stones. [17] Your heart was lifted up because of your beauty; You corrupted your wisdom for the sake of your splendor; I cast you to the ground, I laid you before kings, That they might gaze at you.[18] You defiled your sanctuaries by the multitude of your iniquities, by the iniquity of your trading; Therefore, I brought fire from your midst; It devoured. And I turned you to ashes upon the earth in the sight of all who saw you.[19] All who knew you among the people are astonished at you; You have become a horror, And shall be no more forever" (NIV).

We can notice how great Satan was before he disobeyed God and all he had he still has. Satan lived close to God and in all what God created he was there hence he knows God very well. And because God knew the heart of devil he gave him leadership but he was not happy at all. The devil wanted to take authority in his control. Satan knows that the only way to deceive us is to give us his power so that we should disobey God and he is very wise than us human beings. Other books say his wisdom is thousand times that of human beings. That is why God always say the beginning of wisdom is to fear the Lord. Without God we cannot overcome evil. It is imperative to say that God did not allow the devil to know more about human being because God knew everything and He saw the future and God made a human being in his image without Satan's knowledge. When we read Genesis 1:26-27 "Then God said, 'Let us make man in our image, in our likeness, and let them rule the fish of the sea, and the birds of the air, over the livestock, over the all the earth, and over all the creature that move along the ground,' so God created man in his own image, in the image of God He created him; male and female He created them"(NIV).

The Devil was not happy that God was planning to make man in His own image because to Satan that meant man would be powerful than him. Satan also thought that God will give him authority to look after man as Satan was already in control of other things. If God would have given Satan was wishing chaos would result because devil would have made his own man. So what the Devil challenged God for he was frustrated because he did not have any power to make the human being. Therefore the devil developed hatred on human beings from the beginning and that made him to come and deceive us. Although things were like that God, our heavenly Father warned us not to eat the fruit of the tree at the centre of garden Eden. We never listened to God, because of that Satan took control and the result was deception. But God is love He sent His love and begotten son to die for us, to buy us again with his blood. Hence we become free people and we are God's people. The choice is given unto us to seek the kingdom of God and have everlasting life or die with the devil. Satan destroys God's creation, he destroys us as well, he makes us lose faith in our heavenly Father. Look at us now, we never trust and believe our world is full of competition, suffering, pain and everyone wants to be somebody. This was not God's plan. God wants us to live a life of content, happiness, joy, peace and loving one another.

Satan had a chance to change and God warned him that "what you are planning is bad" but he did not listen or confess. He further went on deceiving other angels and there was war in heaven. As such he was chased from heaven and casted down. Although God casted the devil down, God never destroyed him and it does not mean that he will not destroy him, He will when the right time comes. Revelation 20:10 And the devil that deceived them was cast into the lake of fire and brimstone, where the beast and the false prophet are, and shall be tormented day and night for ever and ever (KJV). The devil and his descendants will be burned and they will be no more sin. Thus; we shall have new heaven and new earth. One day will see all this and will know more how good is Our Father in heaven.

ONE INCH

There was a rich man who was looking for a good place to live along the lake side. And one day He saw the nice place and he went to see it. The owner of the place was a poor man and He just knew that he would buy it at a cheap price. It was just the way as he thought. He bought the area at a very cheap price but the poor man said; "you know, I love this place a lot, you can see yourself, the beach, plum trees, fish, the sun rises, sand, boat and the people as well. So I just want to ask for a favour, may you give me the one inch of your place so that when I come I should not disturb you or pass by your compound." This Rich man joyfully responded; "don't worry I will give it to you look all the area what's one inch to me." This poor man was happy with His one inch. The one inch was a disaster to the rich man who had the whole area. This poor man was taking bad and stinky things and put them in His one inch, such as dead things like cat, dogs, mice, human waste, and poison. His one inch was like a dump he just polluted the whole area. Nobody could come and tell him because he had a simple answer; "this is my area too." We have seen how one inch does in this story.

The same one inch it's the weapon that the devil is using it in our lives. May be in this year we give a devil the one inch of sex, killing, pain to others, stealing, disobedient, temper, lack of respect, lack of confident, selfish, pride, foolishness etc. The one inch has caused excuses: not sharing always wait for others to do that and eating tithe of God in the name of "I don't have enough." Dear friends do not think that we are clever at all when we steal from God it simply means give the Devil one inch. The problem is all we hide from the Lord will pay as a one inch to devil like diseases: cancer, HIV/AIDS, stroke, malaria, BP, etc., bills: hospital bill, rental, electricity, water, school fees, fuel etc. Let us say this little prayer: Dear God forgives us for giving the devil one inch of our lives and he has destroyed us in many ways. Help us next year to give you full of us and we want to see the goodness and happiness of you in the year to come. We declare no one inch of the devil all we need is you God our Father in Heaven.

WELCOMING A DEVIL IS LETTING HIM BUILD A HOME

Luke 11:24-26

24 "When an impure spirit comes out of a person, it goes through arid places seeking rest and does not find it. Then it says, 'I will return to the house I left.' 25 When it arrives, it finds the house swept clean and put in order. 26 Then it goes and takes seven other spirits more wickedly than itself, and they go in and live there. And the final condition of that person is worse than the first" (NIV). Adam and Eve after they ate the fruit their life changed. Therefore, Jesus tells us that when one evil spirit goes out it never leaves forever it comes again. It is the case

since we give it a home and we let it stay, hence when we chase it and it does not find another home then it comes back. Giving a devil a home is easy but to let him go is hard. You cannot take a one month old baby out of your home, saying here is your money for you, if anything come back to me to get more, can that happen? No it can't. The devil is like a one month old baby who never grows in our life so as we still take a good care of it, the devil is immature, disabled and controlling. God's people and good people we have to know our enemy very well before we if are to defeat him. Devil finds a loophole from our parents; Adam and Eve. One thing that he uses most is the insight for he studies us and finds the weakness within us and sometimes he is not sure he just tries like Job's story. Job 1:9-11 "Does Job fear God for nothing?" Satan replied. "Have you not put a hedge around him and his household and everything he has? You have blessed the work of his hands, so that his flocks and herds are spread throughout the land. But now stretch out your hand and strike everything he has, and he will surely curse you to your face" (NIV). It is not always that the devil comes into our life with positive answers sometimes it's a try and error. Proverbs 27:1 "Do not boast about tomorrow, for you do not know what a day may bring" (NIV). The other thing the devil comes with is deception and gives us high expectations, his common approach is "you can do this and you can do that it works." This is seen in Gen 3:1 now the serpent was craftier than any of the wild animals the Lord God had made. He said to the woman, "Did God really say, 'You must not eat from any tree in the garden?'"(NIV) He gives us tricky questions, tests and makes us give wrong answers. Glory to God for His mercies and everlasting love: Deuteronomy 29:29 The secret things belong to the Lord our God, but the things revealed belong to us and to our children forever, that we may follow all the words of this law.

CHAPTER SIX

Do Good Work to Honour God

Colossian 3:22-25 "Slaves, obey your earthly masters in everything; and do it, not only when their eye is on you and to win their favour, but with sincerity of heart and reverence for the Lord. Whatever you do, work at it with all your heart, as working for the Lord, not for men. Since you know that you will receive an inheritance from the Lord as a reward. It is the Lord Christ you are serving. Anyone who does wrong will be repaid for his wrong, and there is no favouritism" (NIV). Same chapter 4; 1 "Masters, provide your slaves with what is right and fair, because you know that you also have a master in heaven" (NIV). Let us do our good work to please our heavenly father, let God reward us with our honest and hardworking. My question is if our earthly masters find favour with us how many times our heavenly Master can find us? Our heavenly Master sees our hearts and our needs while earthly masters just see us only at work. Thus; they do not know us outside the work. God also reminds all earthly masters that He is the Master of masters and we have to fear him first so that our work can achieved. Is the only God who has reward for us, let Him do His job with His love and care on us.

GIVE ME, MAKE ME

Give me, make me. Luke 15:11-32 [11] And he said, A certain man had two sons: [12] And the younger of them said to his father, Father, give me the portion of goods that falleth to me. And he divided unto them his living. [13] And not many days after the younger son gathered all together, and took his journey into a far country, and there wasted his substance with riotous living. [14] And when he had spent all, there arose a mighty famine in that land; and he began to be in want. [15] And he went and joined himself to a citizen of that country; and he sent him into his fields to feed swine. [16] And he would fain have filled his belly with the husks that the swine did eat: and no man gave unto him. [17] And when he came to himself, he said, How many hired servants of my father's have bread enough and to spare, and I perish with hunger! [18] I will arise and go to my father, and will say unto him, Father, I have sinned against heaven, and before thee, [19] And am no more worthy to be called thy son: make me as one of thy hired servants. [20] And he arose, and came to his father. But when he was yet a great way off, his father saw him, and had compassion, and ran, and fell on his neck, and kissed him. [21] And the son said unto him, Father, I have sinned against heaven, and in thy sight, and am no more worthy to be called thy son. [22] But the father said to his servants, Bring forth the best robe, and put it on him; and put a ring on his hand, and shoes on his feet: [23] And bring hither the fatted calf, and kill it; and let us eat, and be merry:

[24] For this my son was dead, and is alive again; he was lost, and is found. And they began to be merry.

[25] Now his elder son was in the field: and as he came and drew nigh to the house, he heard music and dancing. [26] And he called one of the servants, and asked what these things meant. [27] And he said unto him, Thy brother is (has or is?) come; and thy father hath killed the fatted calf, because he hath received him safe and sound. [28] And he was angry, and would not go in: therefore came his father out, and in treated him.

²⁹ And he answering said to his father, Lo, these many years do I serve thee, neither transgressed I at any time thy commandment: and yet thou never gavest me a kid, that I might make merry with my friends: ³⁰ But as soon as this thy son was come, which hath devoured thy living with harlots, thou hast killed for him the fatted calf. ³¹ And he said unto him, Son, thou art ever with me, and all that I have is thine. ³² It was meet that we should make merry, and be glad: for this thy brother was dead, and is alive again; and was lost, and is found, (KJV).

This rich man who had two sons, the young son wanted to have life as the devils words on Job 1:7 from roaming through the earth and going forth" (NIV). Oh good father, he shared the son his property. And the son spent all he had and all things were gone and he even longed to fill his stomach with the pods that the pigs were eating. On verse 17-18 when he came to his senses, he said, "how many of my father's hired men have food to spare, and here I am starving to death! I will set out and go back to my Father and say to Him: father, I have sinned against you. I am no longer worthy to be called your son; MAKE ME like one of your hired men." The Luckiest thing he realized was that he was wrong and he was at a wrong place. Ask yourself are you in the right place or you are in the pods? Do we realize that what we are eating is food for pigs? Then what are we doing or we are happy with it. Let us go back to our Father. Let us realise that it is better to be a hired man in my father's house than eating with pigs.

JESUS IS TESTING OUR FAITH TODAY

MARK 4:35-40 ³⁵ That day when evening came, he said to his disciples, "Let us go over to the other side." ³⁶ Leaving the crowd behind, they took him along, just as he was, in the boat. There were also other boats with him. ³⁷ A furious squall came up, and the waves broke over the boat, so that it was nearly swamped. ³⁸ Jesus was in the stern, sleeping on a cushion. The disciples woke him and said to him,

"Teacher, don't you care if we drown?" [39] He got up, rebuked the wind and said to the waves, "Quiet! Be still!" Then the wind died down and it was completely calm. [40] He said to his disciples, "Why are you so afraid? Do you still have no faith?" (NIV). As we read the story Jesus was sleeping while there was a furious squall and the wave was blocking the boat. Can that happen sleeping in time of trials? What lesson do we learn here? Jesus is teaching us to be strong and calm in the Lord. No matter what, we need to have peace in the Lord and know that He is there for us and He will rescue us in any other way. Jesus wants you and me to call Him when we cannot manage it, He wants us to ask, cry to Him, and he wants us to depend on His name always. May be our problem is unsolved because we are not calling His name. May be you say "God you know everything of me." Although God sees our problems He wants us to do something about it; talk to God about it and He will solve it. Call and tell Him what we want and He is there for us. We can see through the story above that when His disciples called to Jesus He woke up and spoke to the wind and the wind calmed down. Let Jesus rebuke to your trials, problems, and sickness, lonely and to each and every suffering you are passing through today. If we let Jesus speak to us today all the impossible will be possible, let Jesus speak to us, to calm down all the evil power, let Jesus take control in what we speak. In general let God control our lives today. May the good Lord help us know and realise that Jesus died on the cross because of you and me. May the Lord help us to let Jesus speak to each and every way we are passing today to calm down and give us courage.

WHEN GOD HAS ANOTHER PLAN

God's plan does not work in the order we think, it does not work with the knowledge we have. Think of Joseph, He had a very good dream, dream that showed that he would be a ruler someday. And he dreamed when he was little boy, dreams sometimes are hard to understand. Let us highlight Joseph's story before his success, we need to see the challenges he faced: firstly, the brothers did not agree to be ruled by him. Even parents could not bow before their son, Joseph. All this happened because he told them what he dreamed. Most of the times when there are good things, people never listen. Secondly, it was denial, the same brothers created enmity hence they wanted to fight their brother. This happened because they knew that they were the chosen generation and God had chosen Joseph not them. Thirdly, it was harm, war, lies and even a plot of murder. Putting him in a pit while he was alive, this was a half death situation, after that they sold into slavery. Furthermore, Joseph was attempted to sleep with wife of his boss (Potiphar). After that, he was put in prison which meant there was no hope for him to become somebody the way he dreamed.

Finally, when Joseph was in prison he thought that his life was over for nobody seemed to care about him. The relative denied him and being prisoner in a foreign country became very difficult for him to survive. He was relieved one day when he interpreted dreams of two servants and it happened the way he did. He asked the other servant please remember me when you are out. Later the king had troubles with a dream and the servant remembered that Joseph knew how to interpret hence he was called. And from that day Joseph his life changed, in away God remembered Him. Indeed, God's plan does not work with our wisdom and sometimes we pass in tough ways that without faith we can fall in bad ways. Beloved we must not lose hope, stick to the plan of the Lord no matter how long it will take. We pass through all this way for the better tomorrow. Sometimes others can disappoint you in several ways but if you are in the plan of God, He will review himself to you. Faith is the only key to connect with God. Although Joseph passed the long way but the dream was fulfilled and he became the ruler and the redeemer. Remember one more road, one more valley, one more mountain but it will carry us home. Never drawback, let people talk, whatever happens trust in the Lord. Lord knows everything and he blesses accordingly.

CHAPTER SEVEN

God Promises

Genesis 6:13 "So God said to Noah," I am going to put an end to all people, for the earth is filled with violence because of them, I am surely going to destroy both them and the earth"(NIV). We all know this story of the flood filled the earth. Let us just see this verse God wants to destroy the people because of the violence filled on the earth. And at the same time is talking to the man who found favour in God hence he gives Noah a plan to build an ark. God clearly tells Noah all details about the ark like the size and kind of tree(s) to be used. He also tells him to preach to the world that God is going to destroy the people and the earth as well. What do we observe here? God is Love and He is compassion as such He warns the people and also finds the way for them to survive? God did what He said before and he destroyed the earth and the people as well and just kept eight people and all other living creatures. But why did God keep them on earth, why did He not just destroy them and take the righteous ones to heaven as He did with Enoch? We can ask like that but let us not forget our heavenly father is full of promises and He fulfils them. For instance; He promised Adam to fill the Earth and increased in number as sand. And He promised to save His people and sent His one and only beloved son that whosoever believe in Him shall not perish but have everlasting life. And remember God promised to destroy all evil doers and the

God's Mysterious Ways

devil. He is the same God in John 14 who says; He is going to prepare a place and He will come again to take us so that will live with Him forever, if not he would have tell us. He is the same God who tells us in Revelation 3:11 behold I am coming soon, Hold on to what you have, so that non-one will take your crown. Let us hold on to our faith and to our God who is faithful. Heaven is good and it is our home we need to get prepared for it. We shall not be like people in the time of Noah who were there helping the construction of the ark and escorted Noah to salvation. Thus; we should not help others attain salvation yet we do not. We should work for our salvation because it will happen like in the ark whereby eight people were saved. Let us be alert for even during Lot's time it also happened (Lot and his two daughters were saved). We should not be deceived because if one person is righteous God will come for Him. Indeed, when the time comes he will take that person only and destroy the sinners. God wants the people who believe not the ones who merely call themselves Christians. We need to clean our ways everyday of our life because God is on His way to take us home.

WITH GOD

2 Kings 6:1-2 the company of the prophets said to Elisha, 'look the place where we meet with you is too small for us. Let us go to the Jordan, where each of us can get a pole: and let us build a place there for us to live. "And he said "Go"(NIV). We can observe that the prophets were speaking with Elisha about the place they met was very small for them. Now I want everybody here to think of the place we are and with our God. Is the place good, do we fit in? May be our places are very small to meet God or there is no space for God. Take that place as your heart; does God fit in there or not? May be God is failing to fit in because of too much staff that is in there already? Things like what? gossip, pride, killing, worshiping other gods, enemy, witchcraft, failing to keep the holy Sabbath, in short failing to obey God and His promises and commandments. Do we see ourselves that

47

we did not give Lord a place in our hearts? Open your heart and say Lord I might think that I have given a place in my heart, but you are not fitting in because of my sins. God you are the only one who can clean up my mess, I am giving you my heart now use me, fill me and take the control of me today.

2 Kings 6:3-4 Then one of them said, "Won't you please come with your servants?" I will, "Elisha replied. And He went with them (NIV). They went to Jordan and began to cut down trees. In verse one and two we observe that the place was very small and they wanted to do something about it, and now we can see they are going to cut trees to start their construction. And they asked Elisha if he could go with them, and he agreed and they went together. What lesson do we get from this verse? After allowing God to have place in our heart, we need to surrender all to him. For instance; take God to our working places, to our schools, our business, our meetings, interviews and in each and every activity. May be this year we are having many plans in our life, such as: buying cars, great achievements in our business, our careers, model, fashion and many more. Have we involved God? It is never too late, invite God in our plans this year, this month, this week, this day, this hour, this minute, this second we may never regret. Try to take God this year, you may see your tough boss to be nice, you can see more understanding in your things, like school, you can be a better person in every area you are going to be. See more changes in your life this year take God and walk with Him always.

2 Kings 6:5-7 "as one of them was cutting down trees, the iron axe-head fell into the water. "OH, my Lord, "he cried out, "it was borrowed!" The man of God asked, "Where did it fall? "When he showed him the place, Elisha cut a stick and threw it there, and made the iron float. "Lift it out, "he said. Then the man reached out his hand and took it," (NIV). After giving Jesus our hearts then we will walk with Him. Then we have to use Him always, let Him take control now. In the story above there are two things need to be carefully understood.

The iron axe-head fell into the water and the man cried "Oh! it was borrowed." Do we take a good care of someone's property or we do not care? Many people do not care to pay back or to take a good care of someone's property. The Bible teaches us to take a good care of things we borrow. What type of leaders are we if we do not care? What type of light of the world are we, if we do not care? Let us learn from here to take a good care of borrowed things. The second thing I found interesting is when the axe head fell in the water he cried to the right person. Where do we cry to when things are not alright? Let us learn to put our pain to God. We can talk to God even if we are in pain. We must know that the only answer for everything is Jesus, He carried them already at the cross and He knows how to handle them. Avoid crying where you will be confused and disappointed. We can see here the man of God he just asked "show me where" and he float the axe using the stick. Stop crying show God your problem(s) He is waiting from you, to show Him. Show God all your needs let us give God the place and walk with Him this year so that He may float all our needs. Let us cry to Him and show Him all we need. Remember all riches, wealth, peace, love, grace, mercy, and faith belong to our heavenly father. Learn to take our pain to God where there are answers.

GOD WITH US

God is always with us, no matter what He is there and He watches and guides us. In the book of Exodus He tells us that the cloud was with them during the day and the fire was with them during the night. No matter what, He never sleeps or get tired. When Jesus was at the cross, he cried "My God why have you forsaken me". What does this mean? Did God leave Jesus? The answer is No, He did not but it was because of our sins which disturbed Him. This is evident in Isaiah 59:2 which says "But your iniquities have separated you from your God; your sins have hidden his face from you, so that he will not hear" (NIV). Similarly, we cannot hear, listen, obey, understand, and believe in God when we are in sin. Although we are sinners God does not hate us, He still loves us, and He simply hates the sinful nature. Because of that He gives us a choice to leave our sins and ask for forgiveness. He is God of grace but His grace comes to us if we confess our sins and start a new life with Him. God is very clear on this "that if you confess your sins you are my child and I will give you my kingdom and you shall have everlasting life." We have a choice to have everlasting life with God or to be dead forever. Whether we like it or not God will perish sin and He will destroy sin and if you will be in sinful nature He will destroy you together. Make a good choice now, it is very soon, God will put all sinful nature to end. And we will live a wonderful and everlasting life with God.

GOD PROTECTION AMONG US

Today I want us to see how God protects us. 1Kings 14; 4-5 So Jeroboam's wife did what he said and went Ahijah's house in Shiloh. Now Ahijah could not see; his sight was gone because of his age. But the Lord had told Ahijah, "Jeroboam's wife is coming to ask you about her son, for he is ill, and you are to give her such and such an answer. When she arrives, she will pretend to be someone else"(NIV). Sometimes other people go to man of God just to test him and they hide their Identities so that they can tell a lie to him. But if you are a man of God, God will review all secrets to you and even tell you who the real person is and what they want. God will give you answers on how you should handle such people. The devil is a liar he always wants favour and cheating everywhere. For instance He used a certain woman to pretend to be someone just because the prophet was blind and cheat herself that he could not remember her voice hence she lied. We need to be very careful to the people of God. Never cheat and lie. God knows us more than we think and God rewards according to our work not the way we look. The shameful things on verse six are that Ahijah calls her just when he hears the footsteps, how do you feel when the devil makes you feel ashamed. Good people let us not allow the devil fool us. Arise! He always fools us. Let us run to our heavenly Father in order to have good answers and gain our Identity.

GOD COMFORT US

(John 14; 1-4)

Jesus Comforts His Disciples "Do not let your hearts be troubled. You believe in God believe also in me. 2 My Father's house has many rooms; if that were not so, would I have told you that I am going there to prepare a place for you? And if I go and prepare a place for you, I will come back and take you to be with me that you also may be where I am. You know the way to the place where I am going" (NIV). God leads us the way, God gives us His promises, commandment and teaching. He always tells us His plan and the good plan He has for us. Although we are sinners He still gives us his promises that we shall overcome some day. He is coming to take us home. How precious are we? Our Heavenly Father also teaches us a life of heaven our Home. We are learning to live a life of love as our Father is, we learn to forgive, and trust in Him always. The truth is God is love and if we cannot see it now just say a little prayer in our hearts; "Dear God in heaven teach me to know your love, kind, hope, faith, strong and courage." One thing that we can challenge devil is that God is love and is open to us. Keep this and make it your rule and you will work best and soon will reach home. Remember, the day draws near.

CHAPTER EIGHT

How Caring is Our God

Jeremiah 29; 11 "For I know the plan I have for you," declare the Lord, "plan to prosper you and not to harm you, plans to give you hope and future"(NIV). God is a promising God and gives hope, despite how people hate you but God loves you because He knew you before in your mother's womb and He always makes us to be free from fear. He is an understanding God. He controls all things. God clearly shows his good plans for us and plans which give us hope and future. Do you believe this? Yes we should, for He is the same God we say He knows us before we were formed in our mother's womb. And now He says He has good plans for us. God knows us and he blesses us in different ways. He makes smart and one funny thing is look at ourselves everyone has its own face. Sometimes we lose hope and think that there is no other way. And we also say better to be animals, problems make us forget who we are in God's presence. But God is telling us on Jeremiah 31:17 "So there is hope for your future, "declare the Lord" (NIV). Yes as long as God has given us another day there is hope for our future. Things can get tough than before but bear in mind there is hope for your future. God does not lie, let us keep His word in our heart and make it a light in our life hence we will prosper. Trust in the Lord be still and wait for the Lord. Matthew 6:25-33 ²⁵ Therefore I say unto you, Take no thought for your life, what ye shall eat, or what ye shall drink; nor yet for your body, what ye shall put on. Is not the life more than meat, and the body than raiment? [26] Behold the fowls of the air: for they sow not, neither do they reap, nor gather into barns; yet your heavenly Father feedeth them. Are ye not much better than they? [27] Which of you by taking thought can add one cubit unto his stature? [28] And why take ye thought for raiment? Consider the lilies of the field, how they grow; they toil not, neither do they spin: [29] And yet I say unto you, That even Solomon in all his glory was not arrayed like one of these. [30] Wherefore, if God so clothe the grass of the field, which today is, and tomorrow is cast into the oven, shall he not much more clothe you, O ye of little faith? [31] Therefore take no thought, saying, What shall we eat? Or What shall we drink? or, Wherewithal shall we be clothed? [32] (For after all these things do the Gentiles seek:) for your heavenly Father knoweth that ye have need of all these things. [33] But seek ye first the kingdom of God, and his righteousness; and all these things shall be added unto you (KJV).

MIGHTY TO SAVE

Matthew 11:28 "Come to me, all you who are weary and burdened, and I will give you rest" (NIV). Are you weary and burdened? Jesus is calling you today. He is not just calling but His hands are open for everyone and he is not selective. Everyone has heard His invitation and It depends on us to go to Jesus and have rest. My question is have we taken a step to go to Him? Or maybe we are on the line waiting room? Or we have held a ticket waiting for our turn? As I read the calling and welcoming of Jesus that means we will be the first ones to be attend to hence there is no time to waste. Why do we still cry our burdens while Jesus door is open and waiting for us? One day a woman was carrying heavy things and certain man was who was driving said "can I take you in my car so that you can rest" and the woman answered "your very kind young man." He took her but the young man was surprised to see the woman still putting a heavy luggage in her lap. The question is what was the problem with the woman? The problem that the woman had is the same problem we have. In other words, we go to church but we do not change. Jesus died on the cross for you and me but we are still suffering because we do not want Him to give us rest. Little do we know that it is very easy to cry to Jesus than to a friend. Try today to rest in Jesus. If you cry to people, they get used with you and when you go to them frequently, they start discussing and finding fault. However, Jesus will never find fault(s) on us and He will never make feel shamed but He help us. May the good Lord help us to know the real shoulder to cry on.

WHAT TYPE OF TREES ARE WE?

LUKE 13:6-9

He spoke also this parable; A certain man had a fig tree planted in his vineyard; and he came and sought fruit thereon, and found none. Then said he unto the dresser of his vineyard, Behold, these three years I come seeking fruit on this fig tree, and find none: cut it down; why cumbereth it the ground? And he answering said unto him, Lord, let it alone this year also, till I shall dig about it, and dung it: And if it bear fruit, well: and if not, then after that thou shalt cut it down (KJV). This tree depicts how people of today are; we do not bear fruits. God is waiting for us to do His work, to bear good fruits and to do goodwill and follow all of His will and law. Galatians 5:22-23 "But the fruit of the Spirit is love, joy, peace, forbearance, kindness, goodness, faithfulness, gentleness and self-control. Against such things there is no law" (NIV). God wants us to bear good fruits but do you know that God is tired now? Every time He comes to see the tree He sees nothing, not even flowers that show that one day the tree will bear fruits. Why do we live like that, letting our hearts to suffer with hardness and unforgiveness while we are the image of God? In verse seven, the man who took care of vineyard says, "Wait may be next year something will happen." Jesus is always telling God; please wait give them sometime may be they will soften their hearts and bear good fruits. Ask yourself; for how long will God give us some time? May be the three years has passed and we are remaining with one year, maybe we are in the last year, may be we just remain with some months, may be its just a month, may be some weeks, may be a week, may be a day, may be some hours, may be an hour, may be some minutes, or a minute, may be seconds. What are we doing? Hey! Look around, salvation is for everyone and it is your choice not your mother's, Father's, Husband's, wife's, daughter's or son's. That choice is for you and only you. Make a good choice before that opportunity is gone, it will never come again, if we die we will never come back and start again.

HE HIDETH MY SOUL

There was a young girl who was very sick. She was asthmatic since birth. This girl had faith in God and she knew that God is here no matter how long it will take and one day she will be free. Most of the times when she was in pain she heard this song; "He hideth my soul in the cleft of the rock. That shadows a dry, thirsty land; He hideth my life with the depths of His love, And covers me there with His hand, And covers me there with His hand." From this I learned that even in pain God is with us and He is the only one who keep and hide our life. Thus; He is the one who is in charge of our life. Matthew10; 28 "And fear not them which kill the body, but are not able to kill the soul: but rather fear him which is able to destroy both soul and body in hell," (KJV). The verse makes me strong every day of my life because I see many who love God be abused but they stand firm. It's hard to know what they feel unless you are in God's life. God cares for us, in many ways some of which we cannot see with our own eyes but with the knowledge of God.

WHO DO YOU DEPEND ON?

Isaiah 41:10 "So do not fear, for I am with you; do not be dismayed, for I am your God. I will strengthen you and help you; I will uphold you with my righteous right hand" (NIV) There was a certain woman who was traveling, and the day before leaving she said a prayer; "dear God be with me and help this long journey for I depend. She began to sleep and she just received a note and a word, fear not for I am with you and the note was written - Isaiah 41:10. When she woke up she opened the bible and straight away it was the verse on the note. Do you believe that God gives us strength? From that day the woman went through tough life experiences. During all the painful and hard life experiences she was passing through, she was the conqueror. When she was passing through that, God was telling her, reminding her; do not fear I am with you. When you have God you will pass through the road, valleys, mountains, fire even winter full of snow. God changes your way. God makes you strong in every way of life. I can give you example of how life works with God: you are walking a fifteen minutes' walk distance and you for five minutes. Ask yourself "how did I make it, what happened?" God is a director.

Have you ever been to the place where people prepare to fight with you? And at the end they are fighting one another. Have you ever been given a drink or a food with poison or glasses on it? And everybody just look at you "let her drink she has to die." And you drink or eat it but hold on to your peace still getting strong. May be somebody has ever played with your cosmetics and put some poison so that can react and destroy your skin. Then nothing happens, in fact your skin just works better and look softer than before. Why am I telling all these things today? When God controls your life everything works best. Most of the times your enemies come with strange questions like; how was your journey? Then you ask yourself "how did they know I was going somewhere?" And sometimes they ask you what lotion you use? "I think I use the same like yours but my skin is dry." Sometimes

God do it for us without having a testimony but you may wonder why people hate us? They hate what you have and who you depend on. It is true in Luke 10:19 it says; "I have given you authority to trample on snakes and scorpions and to overcome all the power of the enemy; nothing will harm you" (NIV). God has numerous ways for protecting us. God makes things to work but sometimes we are praising our self-forget that there was God behind everything. Like the Israelites they passed through the red sea with pressure from the Egyptians who were coming; everyone wanted to be saved. At the end God just told Moses, strike the rod again and water came back to normal, that is when they realized the good works of God. We have to be happy when we are passing through hard times with God, because that is the only way to thank God and see how wonderful His deeds are in our life. It is for His Glory.

CHAPTER NINE

When God Says Yes, Who Can Say No?

Matthew 6:10 Thy kingdom come, Thy will be done in earth, as it is in heaven. (KJV) No matter how? No matter when? No matter why? No matter who? No matter what? No matter where? In all questions we can asks but when God says no its no or when God say yes is yes. There were soldiers guarding Jesus body, but when on the third day He rose again and left them there. Jesus went first to present Himself to His Father and got His approval. He is the living God. In other words, if you walk in the kingdom of God His Will, will definitely be done from heaven and the approval will come to us. The Devil fails many times because most of the times Heaven's approval is not there. Trust in the Lord always and let His will happen in your life. Let God give you guidance, authority and power. His love guides our daily life. If God is with us, we will pass in all situations, the devil can surround us left, right and centre but with God we will pass and when we pass we will know that it was not us but our loving Father.

ARE WE A HEAD OR TAIL? WHO ARE YOU?

Deuteronomy 28:13 "And the LORD shall make thee the head, and not the tail; and thou shalt be above only, and thou shalt not be beneath; if that thou hearken unto the commandments of the LORD thy God, which I command thee this day, to observe and to do them," (KJV). That's it the Lord will make you a head-but there is a condition which is if you pay attention to His commandments. This verse shows that we can be heads, bright, brave, wise, smart and good leader if we pay attention and do the God's will. The point I want us to see now is if we will not do as God's commandments stipulate and His will, we are tails. Ask yourself today do we fear God? And do we do God's will or we are tail? Whether we like it or not if do not have God in our lives we are tails. Why am I saying so? Look around unfaithful relationships, we never use head to see love but we use a tail. Why do we believe in sex and make it ungodly. The world is in chaos because we are tail we do not want God control His earth. We do not know that if we listen to God's commandments, all our problems will be solved. We are tails in many ways for we put God aside. The world is full of lies because we do not want to be a head the way our God wants us to be. We can be leaders, designers, specialists, Doctors, Professors, Teachers, Advisers and many more, but if we do not have God, we are still tails. While if you are viewed as nothing; without being married, poor, been giving names, others laugh and make you to be unknown but if you have God you are still the head. It is better to have nothing in the world that people can point at but have God. This implies that you are more than those that have everything in the world. Sometimes it looks awkward if you have God, but it does not take much time when God turns things. God knows that you are on the safe side, no matter how you can be bulled, abused, laugh, played in many ways. You can feel pain and sometimes feel that you are wasting time but there is no wasting time with God. And He promises to be there for us always and tells us every day that we shall not fear because He is with us. He knows that sometimes we pass tough ways but remember thou shall not fear. Trust in the Lord and know that he is our savoir and our God. It is always good to pray: Thank you Heavenly, Precious, Gracious, Wonderful and Merciful Father for this beautiful night. You have been with us from Morning throughout the day up to this time. Not because we deserve this but it is your mercy and undisputed Love. Father during the day we have sinned against you we ask for you forgiveness. Father abides with us this silent night. There are a lot of things which can destroy our lives and property. Thus; protect us from evil forces. Dear father we thank you for speaking to us throughout the day in different messages and Evangelist. Bless those who are taking your word to the world. Through the name of Jesus who died on cross I pray. Amen

POWER IN THE BLOOD

There is power in the blood of Jesus, is this true? If it is, then why are we busy sacrificing and shade blood of innocent soul? Leviticus 17:11"for the life of the body is in its blood. I have given you the blood on the altar to purify you, making you right with the LORD. It is the blood, given in exchange for a life that makes purification possible" (NIV). God clearly teaches us that there is life of the body in its blood, and that blood purifies us. There is only one blood which can purify us and is the blood of Jesus. It is the blood of Jesus that washes our sins, that heals us, that gives us hope and faith, it is the blood of Jesus that hears our prayers and make us holy, is the blood of Jesus that gives us grace, mercy, lighting our ways and blessings. Is the blood of Jesus that makes us strong, trust in Him and have no fear? Then who taught us to shade innocent blood so that we can be rich? Who taught us to kill somebody to take his position? Why do women abort? What is blood as for today's lesson? Blood is life. We have no right to take somebody's blood (life) no matter what. Jesus already shades His blood for us and is the only powerful blood that works best in our lives in all our ways. If we have ever taken somebody's life in any other way, we need to ask for God's forgiveness and be free. Dear God forgive us for taking things in our hands, teach us to trust in you always.

CHAPTER TEN

Testimonies

THE JOURNERY

There was a certain lady who was going abroad to do her education. She had everything that was needed for her education and her family was financially stable as well. But this God fearful woman said a little prayer to God "I might think I have everything but God I just want to have you and you alone." And she took her money and gave tithe to God and told God that one day all this will be gone. But one thing God I ask from you is to supply my needs; I should have food on my table, clothes to keep me warmth and a good place to sleep most of all, give me peace and never show to the world how poor I am. Until now God is doing what she asked Him and she has a good life. Suffice to say that life is hard without God in simple words, is just a total mess. What did you ask God when you saw the downfall of your life? Tell God what you need and He will do what He did to the Israel's when they were in wilderness. Do not hesitate, tell God and he will help you, for He is rich. Give God time to teach us and heal us and do His work in our lives.

ENCOURAGE ONE ANOTHER CHILDREN OF GOD

There was a woman who survived cancer for three times. Firstly, it was a tumor which she struggled with in her stomach and she went for surgery after years it came again and it was in the uterus and she survived but she lost her uterus. The last time it came again and that time it was in her voice code and she was about to lose her voice but a miracle happened she survived. We can see how God worked on her life. This woman did not stop there she helped a family which were HIV positive. Worse still they had a baby who was supposed to be breast fed. She helped the family in prayers and gave them faith to hold on to God. That is about that woman but what do we do when our loved ones are in trouble? What do we do when God has shown His power and impossible things to be possible? Do we let accept them in the name of its part of life? Do we give faith to them, or we just think of running away from them. What do we do? The devil is the liar, he wants to shut our mouth, he wants us to stop believing that God loves us and He cares for us. The devil wants to steal our pride, faith, strong, courage, and confidents in the Lord. We have to hold hands together as children of God. We have to support each other and carry on with our faith and spread the good news of our Heavenly Father. Jesus tells us in John 14 "do not let our hearts be troubled," let us believe in Him hold on to your faith. God do everything for a purpose; remember He has a good plan for us. Stand firm, if God allows such hard and painful things in our life that means he trusts us and He believes that will make it through. Do not forget He did the same things with Job. We should Thank God for all that and thank Him for believing and trusting us.

WOMAN OF FAITH

There was a woman who travelled from her country to another country with the Husband and the kids. They did this to start their life anew because one of the husband's family members was over controlling them precisely, the mother-in-law. It worked during first days later the Husband became a very abusive and controlling. Sometimes we do not know that the Devil is the one we are feeding and carrying in our back. The husband was abusive because he was the evil man he hated the woman because He feared God. This man was forcing the woman to take drugs. He frequently told the wife that "she has to stop praying since according to him she was praying too much hence they were not enjoying pleasures of life." Whenever he came home he would ask the woman what she was doing. Surely, this man made the wife's life like living in the bottle. In addition, the man published the wife's dreams and visions without her knowledge. God knows that sometimes the devil wants to block our communication with Him hence he fight for us. To worsen the situation the man left the wife with a one month old baby girl and run away with the other two boys.

The devil is a liar, he run the woman with a one month old baby and also knew that the woman had no documents for stay in that country as she was using a spouse visa and it would expire very soon. The man wrote a letter to the immigration lying that they planned to go home with his wife. Because the woman did not follow him, his mother was looking after the children. They children were all fine and happy and he employed a babysitter for the boys. All of a sudden, the man left the kids with his mother. Indeed, for second time the man also abandoned his children and went to another country and got married there. Definitely, God was angry with the man's behaviour. Jeremiah 29:11 For I know the thoughts that I think toward you, saith the Lord, thoughts of peace, and not of evil, to give you an expected end (KJV). Let us see how God worked in this woman, she had a scholarship, new house, car, above all she had her kids back and she lived happy after. No matter how the Devil walk in front of you, abuse you, believe and know one thing; God is bigger and He has plans for you. Our God will never leave or forsake us, He is our God.

YOUR FAITH HAS HEALED YOU

Mark 5:34 He said to her, "Daughter, your faith has healed you. Go in peace and be freed from your suffering" (NIV). Why did most of the times Jesus said your faith has healed or saved you? It was hard to understand until I met my best friend. This woman motivates me in many ways. She was infected by HIV and AIDS since 2002, she was very ill and she just lost her handsome baby boy, and the Husband was afraid. So he took her to her village thinking that she would soon die. He did that so that he could not find it difficult to transport her remains for he was poor. The other reason was that he wanted her relatives to see her before something terrible happened to her. We missed her until one day my mother asked the husband where she was. And he gave an explanation as above, however my mother did not agree with his explanation. As such, my mother and other church members arranged transport for him to get his wife. We took a very good care of her and as time went by, she became fine. At that time I was a very little girl and I just told her "I love you so much and you have to forget what happened and be who you are above all, have faith in God."

As I said she lost the Baby and she tried the second time, this time was a baby girl and she lost her again. However, this did not make her lose faith so she tried again and the baby died as usual. Likewise, her faith was still alive, then she became pregnant again and people talked; "do you want to die? What are you thinking, you are infected and now you just wasting your power through delivery and you still doing it, just accept, God does want you to have a child." Then she told God "I will never give up and I will try again and you have to help me and shame the devil." A miracle happened, she had a baby girl and another miracle happened she breast fed her baby until the girl was two years old and never infected, and she is very strong girl till now. She was very happy mother. And it happened again she was pregnant. This triggered questions in her; what is it? God I said I wanted one baby God do you want me to die? But it was a big miracle, she had a baby boy and now the HIV positive is just history. She used to tell me that only God takes a good care of her. She is health strong since she does exercise. She has a farm and it's a long distance such that when I go with her I usually say "I am tired we have to stop" yet she does not complain the distance. She has faith and strong faith for that matter. This is evident as she does not know how to read and write but she is able to preach, she memorises verses and she always tell you stories in the Bible exactly as they are. In need to mention that most of the times when I am depressed, she comforts me by giving me a story to read from the bible. God is mysterious, may be you have a big problem, diseases and sometimes you see that there is no hope. Yes, in the world there is no hope but if you open your eyes and ears to allow God to work on you, you will be fine and healed in Jesus Name. No matter how what you going through but when God says we shall overcome then we shall, Trust in the Lord for His love endure forever.

HOW GOD MYSTERIOUS WAYS WORK IN OUR DAILY LIFE

There was a certain Lady, who made a covenant with Lord that she will never sleep with any man before marriage, and God grant her wish. Although things were like that there were temptations along the way. This young lady was a God fearing woman; she trusted God in all situations. And God was always there for her and she put everything she had in the name of the Lord and her proud came from the Lord. One day something happened when she was with her Boyfriend. They started touching each other and the lady just said "God help me my body is weak take my control Lord." And the phone rang. God will make away and the man said pick up your phone. It had been happening until the man one day decided to switch off her phone. Yes the phone was off but it rang again until the man said ok I will follow your faith. You can see how God works. Here was a phone that God used, God has thousand ways to guide, ride, protect and taking a good care of us.1 Chronicles 29:11 "Yours, O Lord, is the greatness and the power and the glory and the victory and the majesty, for all that is in the heavens and in the earth is yours. Yours is the kingdom, O Lord, and you are exalted as head above al" (NIV). Give God what you have and you will live a safest life ever, you will see His goodness in all your way. And when you are passing through difficult ways which by yourself you cannot overcome, God will use his weapons to protect you. Indeed, He will never lead us into temptation as we invite Him in our daily life.

GOD OUR SAVIOUR

When I was at secondary school I saw God's mysterious ways in me. I was repeating my O level so I had to go to another school. My new school was a girls and boys school but from my primary school to secondary I had been attending girl's schools only. It was a boarding school and everything was new and the school was in rural area. At the school there were a lot of teasing and bullying. So it was very difficult for me to adapt to the environment but I had to. Psalms18:1-2 "I love you, O Lord, my strength. The Lord is my rock, fortress and my deliver; my God is my rock, in whom I take refuge. He is my shield and the horn of my salvation, my stronghold." I saw God being my strength, my rock, fortress, my deliver and my shield. One day I was chatting with my friend so it was a girl talk; the topic was having a boyfriend on campus. I said I could not have a boyfriend on campus and another girl was listening and she told my enemies who changed the story then told boys on campus. So the boys were so furious and wanted to deal with me. They surrounded my class room during a lunch break. I asked for God's help because I knew that there was no other help. God was on my side, and all of a sudden came another boy who was so strong at the campus and everyone feared him, he took me and walked with me. Everyone was afraid of him and that was how I was rescued, I said God help me and I was safe. God will fight for you if you ask for his help.

Then girls said "if the boys leave you like that not us" so they called me to the discipline room where they wanted to deal with me. They called me and forced me to seat on the floor. They asked me if I said that I will not have a boyfriend on campus and I admitted. I justified that it was simply an opinion. Then they allowed me to go and sleep. As I was going to bed other girls said "how could they leave her just like that." That group of girls who were not happy came to my bed when I was sleeping and they pulled water on my bed. God rescued me again I was using a mosquito net on my bed but God used that net to keep water. Indeed, not even a drop of water came inside my bed where I was sleeping. They were amazed of what happened and they said "look at her she is not wet and no water on her bed." God is our saviour and He is always our help in time of trouble. Psalm 110:1 The Lord says to my Lord: "sit at my right hand until I make your enemies a footstool for your feet" (NIV). It came a time when God honoured me. There was a time when another girl fell sick and she needed help, everyone was just looking at her without giving help. She was the girl who talked bad things about me. I helped her and after she got well she came to me to confess. There was another girl who said bad things to me. One day she wanted to go somewhere near my home so I called her and said you can sleep to my home and I took her there and gave her a good hospitality which made her confess everything she had done to me. Certainly, if you sit on the right hand of God, He will make our enemies to be our footstool. You may have problems with others but stay in the right hand with God until God do something for you. There are some enemies for you but let God work for your life. Ask God to help others who hate you. God fight for us and will never leave or forsake us.

CHAPTER ELEVEN

Do Not Judge as You Judge

Matthew 7:1 Judge not, that ye be not judged (KJV). This verse is very tough nowadays, we always walk with some people who act as makers to others. Sometimes we do not see our faults we always see others'. Thus; we think that we are faultless. Certainly, we hide our problems but solve and judge others.

Everything that happens in somebody we are good at finding solutions as if we know everything. Sometimes some people fear and trust God and when things are not working for them we find faults in God. You can say many things and sometimes taking God's law to judge others but your time shall come when you will be judged accordingly. People of God stop judging, stop being Jews, philistines of the time of Jesus. Stop causing harm to others. If God is making your way smooth, then it is time for you to praise Him and say thank you Lord. If your fellow Christians are in trouble, be with them in prayers. Matthew 5Vs 43-48 "Ye have heard that it hath been said, Thou shalt love thy neighbour, and hate thine enemy. But I say unto you, Love your enemies, bless them that curse you, do good to them that hate you, and pray for them which despitefully use you, and persecute you; That ye may be the children of your Father which is in heaven: for he maketh his sun to rise on the evil and on the good, and sendeth rain on the just and on the unjust. For if ye love them which love you, what reward have ye? do not even the publicans the same? And if ye salute your brethren only, what do ye more than others? do not even the publicans so? Be ye therefore perfect, even as your Father which is in heaven is perfect." (KJV) We need to learn to be humble as our Heavenly father, Let love judge, let God do His on work with His power. You can see here even the sun rises to everyone, others achieve a lot while others not, even rain falls to everyone the same rain, kill, and the same rain make others being homeless, the same rain is the blessing to others. Let me tell you something, evil people always judge others. Galatians 6 vs7-8 be not deceived; God is not mocked: for whatsoever a man soweth, that shall he also reap. For he that soweth to his flesh shall of the flesh reap corruption; but he that soweth to the Spirit shall of the Spirit reap life everlasting" (NIV).

WITH GOD WE CAN LOOK LIKE PRISONERS BUT WE ARE FREE

Acts 16:25-28 "And at midnight Paul and Silas prayed, and sang praises unto God: and the prisoners heard them. And suddenly there was a great earthquake, so that the foundations of the prison were shaken: and immediately all the doors were opened, and every one's bands were loosed. And the keeper of the prison awaking out of his sleep, and seeing the prison doors open, he drew out his sword, and would have killed himself, supposing that the prisoners had been fled. But Paul cried with a loud voice, saying, Do thyself no harm: for we are all here," (KJV). As we read this story when Paul and Silas were in prison, they were just happy and they still trusted and believed in God. They even had their time with God in singing and praising God. In the process of their prayers, something terrible happened; a violent earthquake. We may wonder what type of earthquake was that, which opened doors and loosen chains. There was an opportunity for them to run away but they never run away and they were still in the prison cells bounded to chains. Even when the world tries to pull us down so that it can prove that we are wrong but if we have God all things will be fine. We can see even the world showed that Paul and Silas were prisoners but it was the same as far as God was concerned. In other words, they were free as evident from opening of the doors and loosen of the chains. When the guard saw that, he was about to kill himself. By implication we would say that the guard was the one who was the prisoner although it is portrayed that he was free man. This is on the basis that he did not have Jesus who is our saviour. Indeed, if we have no Jesus we are prisoners and if we have Jesus we are free people. It does not matter where we are or our identity, nationality, citizenship, occupation, popularity or what so ever we think. People! People! My fellow People time is ticking this leadership, popularity, technological things, fashion and modelling, porch life will never save us not even. They just buy our time, and they will never make us free people hence we shall remain prisoners. You can find him anywhere and let Him be your guide. If you have God in your heart, it will never cost you anything like going for the TV shows, counselling, rehab, yoga, and any other solution to make life better. God is bigger than all your problems and is the best teacher, Father, leader and He is love. And His judgement is perfect than any other.

DO NOT LOVE THE WORLD 1 JOHN 2; 15-17

1 John 2:15-17 King James Version (KJV) [15] "Love not the world, neither the things that are in the world. If any man love the world, the love of the Father is not in him. [16] For all that is in the world, the lust of the flesh, and the lust of the eyes, and the pride of life, is not of the Father, but is of the world. [17] And the world passeth away, and the lust thereof: but he that doeth the will of God abideth for ever." God is warning us, not to love the world or anything in the world. Why should we not love the world? It cannot make sense, we live in the world and this is our home since we have never been in another

planet. Indeed, some things make sense with God only. God created us and gave us this earth as our home. And He also gave us authority to control all his creation but from nowhere everything changed. Yes everything changed because we gave the devil a right to control and destroy our life. But since God is love He promised to take us to a new home through Jesus Christ. No wonder He tells that the earth is not our home we are just passing by. What we love most is what we please and praise. For instance, the one who made a car wanted to minimize the distance, but the idea of having a car is now viewed as posh lifestyle. Look at computers every now and then things are changing, windows vista, window XP, windows 7 now windows 8, windows 8.1. See in world of dressing fashion it's on high demand. Everyone wants to have a standard life. Look outside everything is creative. We can have everything but bear in mind to thank God for giving us all that. Remember without God its lust and sin.

CHAPTER TWELVE

Are Visitors Welcomed In Our Homes?

Do we invite visitors in our home? What type of visitors do we invite? Let see together how the other woman in the bible became blessed because of her welcoming spirit. 2 Kings 4:8-17 [8] One day Elisha went to Shunem. And a well-to-do woman was there, who urged him to stay for a meal. So whenever he came by, he stopped there to eat. [9] She said to her husband, "I know that this man who often comes our way is a holy man of God. [10] Let's make a small room on the roof and put in it a bed and a table, a chair and a lamp for him. Then he can stay there whenever he comes to us." [11] One day when Elisha came, he went up to his room and lay down there. [12] He said to his servant Gehazi, "Call the Shunammite." So he called her, and she stood before him. [13] Elisha said to him, "Tell her, 'You have gone to all this trouble for us. Now what can be done for you? Can we speak on your behalf to the king or the commander of the army?'" She replied, "I have a home among my own people." [14] "What can be done for her?" Elisha asked. Gehazi said, "She has no son, and her husband is old." [15] Then Elisha said, "Call her." So he called her, and she stood in the doorway. [16] "About this time next year," Elisha said, "you will hold a son in your arms." "No, my lord!"

she objected. "Please, man of God, don't mislead your servant!"[17] But the woman became pregnant, and the next year about that same time she gave birth to a son, just as Elisha had told her"(NIV). God wants us to be like this woman who forgot her needs and welcomed a man of God in her house, building him a home to stay. What a surprises is that the woman never kept the man of God for a favour not even one. She was happy to have him in her home that was enough to her. God wants us to invite him in our lives, in our heart, in our home, in our working places, whatever we do and where ever we go, He wants us to invite him. God wants us to build a home for Him. If we just invite God in our home He will give our needs in our day to day life. Try it this time never ask Him just invite him in our lives and we will see our life changing and will be granted all important needs in our life. Ask God today to show us our needs let heaven talk about us today. Let God think for us and we will be blessed than ever before.

HUMBLE YOURSELF

2 Kings 5:1-6 now Naaman was commander of the army of the king of Aram. He was a great man in the sight of his master and highly regarded, because through him the LORD HAD GIVEN VICTORY TO ARAM. HE WAS A VALIANT SOLDIER, BUT HE HAD LEPROSY. [2] Now bands of raiders from Aram had gone out and had taken captive a young girl from Israel, and she served Naaman's wife. [3] She said to her mistress, "If only my master would see the prophet who is in Samaria! He would cure him of his leprosy."

[4] Naaman went to his master and told him what the girl from Israel had said. [5] "By all means, go," the king of Aram replied. "I will send a letter to the king of Israel." So Naaman left, taking with him ten talents of silver, six thousand shekels of gold and ten sets of clothing. [6] The letter that he took to the king of Israel read: "With this letter I

am sending my servant Naaman to you so that you may cure him of his leprosy," (NIV).

Naaman was a commander of the king of Aram and he was a great man in the sight of his master. But Naaman had leprosy. In Naaman's house there was a little girl who was a servant and she told her mistress about the man of God in her home Israel in Samaria. What made girl talk about the man of God while she was a servant there? There are two things; one that means she raised that girl in a well-mannered way. The family welcomed her in their home, that was why the girl tried to find the solution to the sickness. Secondly, that means she never hid her identity and she spread the word of God anywhere despite being a slave. How do we live with the people who work for us? Do we treat them well, do we know that those people are the ones who can help us or destroy us? We need to live and respect other at all times as Naaman did since the foreign girl saved his life. 2 Kings 5:7-14 ⁷ As soon as the king of Israel read the letter, he tore his robes and said, "Am I God? Can I kill and bring back to life? Why does this fellow send someone to me to be cured of his leprosy? See how he is trying to pick a quarrel with me!" ⁸ When Elisha the man of God heard that the king of Israel had torn his robes, he sent him this message: "Why have you torn your robes? Have the man come to me and he will know that there is a prophet in Israel." ⁹ So Naaman went with his horses and chariots and stopped at the door of Elisha's house. ¹⁰ Elisha sent a messenger to say to him, "Go, wash yourself seven times in the Jordan, and your flesh will be restored and you will be cleansed." ¹¹ But Naaman went away angry and said, "I thought that he would surely come out to me and stand and call on the name of the LORD his God, wave his hand over the spot and cure me of my leprosy. ¹² Are not Abana and Pharpar, the rivers of Damascus, better than all the waters of Israel? Couldn't I wash in them and be cleansed?" So he turned and went off in a rage.¹³ Naaman's servants went to him and said, "My father, if the prophet had told you to do some great thing, would you not have done it? How much more, then, when he tells you, 'Wash and be cleansed'!"

¹⁴ So he went down and dipped himself in the Jordan seven times, as the man of God had told him, and his flesh was restored and became clean like that of a young boy"(NIV).

There are some people in life who always think that they can do anything by themselves, see how the King of Israel handled things. Thus; he handled everything in His hands forgetting that some God's servant were able to do things he could not. He changed his stand when Elisha reviewed himself and said "let them come." No matter what, the word of God cannot fail because others do not allow us to spread it. We should let God's work in His way to spread His words. What a surprise when they went to Elisha's home, Elisha gave Naaman a word "go and wash yourself in Jordan River seven times." And Naaman never saw Elisha but a massager. Naaman was a commander, he just sent his solders to work and they did, but he did not want him to be told in that way. He was looking for full attention from Elisha, precisely he wanted Elisha to visit him but it did not happen that way. God does the same way to us, we never see Him but if we trust Him and have faith everything work best. When God wants to do anything to us, He will never consider where we are or the proper time that will suit us. Naaman was looking for a good way for him to get better and Naaman thought that his healing was from the river but it was so His healing was from himself, what God wanted him to humble himself. Our thinking is different with God's thinking. Sometimes we need others to convince us just as Naaman's servant convinced him and he listened to him and went and washed in Jordan. What a wonderful thing Naaman listened to his servant despite their ranks. Do we do that to others when they are down? Sometimes it is better to do when God commands anything. Consider what Naaman did, he dipped himself in Jordan River for seven times his flesh restored and her skin changed as a young boy. Never use your logic, science, wisdom and power. Our thinking is not God's thinking. He always has a good way and He never consults anyone. Stop using your senses when God says something. Indeed, we need God's guidance always.

ARE WE LIKE GEHAZI WHO WANT PAYMENT WHEN GOD HAS DONE TO OTHERS?

2 King5: 15-27 Then Naaman and all his attendants went back to the man of God. He stood before him and said, "Now I know that there is no God in the entire world except in Israel. So please accept a gift from your servant." [16] The prophet answered, "As surely as the LORD LIVES, WHICH I SERVE, I WILL NOT ACCEPT A THING." AND EVEN THOUGH NAAMAN URGED HIM, HE REFUSED. [17] "If you will not," said Naaman, "please let me, your servant, be given as much earth as a pair of mules can carry, for your servant will never again make burnt offerings and sacrifices to any other god but the LORD. [18] But may the LORD FORGIVE YOUR SERVANT FOR THIS ONE THING: WHEN MY MASTER ENTERS THE TEMPLE OF RIMMON TO BOW DOWN AND HE IS LEANING ON MY ARM AND I HAVE TO BOW THERE ALSO—WHEN I BOW DOWN IN THE TEMPLE OF RIMMON, MAY THE LORD FORGIVE YOUR SERVANT FOR THIS." [19] "Go in peace," Elisha said. After Naaman had traveled some distance, [20] Gehazi, the servant of Elisha the man of God, said to himself, "My master was too easy on Naaman, this Aramean, by not accepting from him what he brought. As surely as the LORD LIVES, I WILL RUN AFTER HIM AND GET SOMETHING FROM HIM." [21] So Gehazi hurried after Naaman. When Naaman saw him running toward him, he got down from the chariot to meet him. "Is everything all right?" he asked.

[22] "Everything is all right," Gehazi answered. "My master sent me to say, 'Two young men from the company of the prophets have just come to me from the hill country of Ephraim. Please give them a talent of silver and two sets of clothing.'" [23] "By all means, take two talents," said Naaman. He urged Gehazi to accept them, and then tied up the two talents of silver in two bags, with two sets of clothing. He gave them to two of his servants, and they carried them ahead of Gehazi. [24] When Gehazi came to the hill, he took the things from the servants and put them away in the house. He sent the men away and they left.

[25] When he went in and stood before his master, Elisha asked him, "Where have you been, Gehazi?" "Your servant didn't go anywhere," Gehazi answered. [26] But Elisha said to him, "Was not my spirit with you when the man got down from his chariot to meet you? Is this the time to take money or to accept clothes—or olive groves and vineyards, or flocks and herds, or male and female slaves? [27] Naaman's leprosy will cling to you and to your descendants forever, Then Gehazi went from Elisha's presence and his skin was leprous—it had become as white as snow"(NIV). Has God done anything to us or he has not done anything to us before? If He has never done, ask Him to do it now so that we can witness. Naaman witnessed himself after he saw what the Lord had done to him. Naaman wanted to give gifts to Elisha but Elisha rejected it. Although Naaman encouraged him to accept but he said "as surely the Lord lives, he will not take one." Elisha allowed Naaman to go in peace. Nevertheless, Gehazi saw the things was so precious to him and thought that with those things his life might change. He also thought that we will lie to Naaman saying "Elisha sent him to follow Naaman" he assumed that when Naaman hears that it is Elisha, he would give him all the gifts. Naaman gave Gehazi what he wanted to give Elisha hence Gehazi was happy and knew that the plan worked and he will run away from Elisha. What type of people are we? Particularly, nowadays when we work for God because of money not His kingdom's sake. Gehazi planned to run away from him because Elisha wanted to live poor life with the word of God but Gehazi did not want to live as Elisha so he decide to run away from Elisha and followed Naaman and lied that Elisha asked him to take the gift from Naaman. But Elisha asked Gehazi where he went, Gehazi responded that he never went anywhere and Elisha told him that his spirit was with him when the man got down from chariot to his way home. The spirit of God follows us, we can cheat others but God will count it as sin in His eyes. Like the way Elisha asked Gehazi "is this the right time to take this from them." Ask the same yourself the question; is it the right time to steal from people in the name of the Lord? Surely, it is the right time to seek God's kingdom. From that moment Gehazi

took all the leprous that Naaman had and Gahazi's was worse in his life time. Do not let blessings of others be affected because you steal them. Sometimes we may think that God gives through what we steal from others. All things we obtained through bad ways will pay for them. Thus; we will be punished. Let us be happy when others are blessed and we should wait for the right time when Lord will bless us. We are all God's children and He has many blessings for us more than we think but we miss God's blessings because of stealing. Like Jacob God waited for him to confess his sin and gave him his blessings. Most of the times we are the ones we make God to delay us, because of our behaviour(s). May the good Lord help us to have patience on him.

JESUS VISIT US THE WAY WE ARE

John 4:1-15. Now Jesus learned that the Pharisees had heard that he was gaining and baptizing more disciples than John. — ² although in fact it was not Jesus who baptized, but his disciples. ³ So he left Judea and went back once more to Galilee. ⁴ Now he had to go through Samaria. ⁵ So he came to a town in Samaria called Sychar, near the plot of ground Jacob had given to his son Joseph. ⁶ Jacob's well was there, and Jesus, tired as he was from the journey, sat down by the well. It was about noon. ⁷ When a Samaritan woman came to draw water, Jesus said to her, "Will you give me a drink?" ⁸ (His disciples had gone into the town to buy <u>food</u>.) ⁹ The Samaritan woman said to him, "You are a Jew and I am a Samaritan woman. How can you ask me for a drink?" (For Jews do not associate with Samaritans. ¹⁰ Jesus answered her, "If you knew the <u>gift</u> of God and who it is that asks you for a drink, you would have asked him and he would have given you living water."¹¹ "Sir," the woman said, "you have nothing to draw with and the well is deep. Where can you get this living water? ¹² are you greater than our father Jacob, who gave us the well and drank from it himself, as did also his sons and his livestock?"¹³ Jesus answered, "Everyone who drinks this water will be thirsty again, ¹⁴ but whoever drinks the water I give them will never thirst. Indeed, the water I give them will become in them a spring of water welling up to eternal life."[15] The woman said to him, "Sir, give me this water so that I won't get thirsty and have to keep coming here to draw water" (NIV). Jesus had a mission of meeting this woman. The woman went and drew water in the noon time, the time that every woman was supposed to cook lunch for the family. Surprisingly, she was alone, in the past years when women went to drew water they went with a company so that they could sit and talk. This woman was causing problems in the Samaria for she was snatching her friend's husbands hence she had no friend. There is a problem when we create a space and have line to devil in our lives; it's when we are creating danger zone in our life. Why am I saying this? This woman was using the same way she snatched men from her friend. Thus, men found her in the well at noon because they knew that the wives were in there homes. On this day she met a strange man, Jesus who started begging her water as all men did. She answered the way she answered all men. With her sweet talk. Let us see how Jesus handled this lady. He just told the woman what she wanted in her life and he added that he would give her water that she would never have thirsty again. The woman was happy thinking that not even one woman would come and bother her again since she will have this man and he will give her the water as such, she will never come there again and look for water.

Now the story will change let us see Jonh4:16 -26 [16] He told her, "Go, call your husband and come back." [17] "I have no husband," she replied. Jesus said to her, "You are right when you say you have no husband. [18] The fact is, you have had five husbands, and the man you now have is not your husband. What you have just said is quite true." [19] "Sir," the woman said, "I can see that you are a prophet. [20] Our ancestors worshiped on this mountain, but you Jews claim that the place where we must worship is in Jerusalem."[21] "Woman," Jesus replied, "believe me, a time is coming when you will worship the Father neither on this mountain nor in Jerusalem. [22] You Samaritans worship what you do not know; we worship what we do know, for salvation is from the Jews. [23] Yet a time is coming and has now come when the true worshipers will worship the Father in the Spirit and in truth, for they are the kind of worshipers the Father seeks. [24] God is spirit, and his worshipers must worship in the Spirit and in truth." [25] The woman said, "I know that Messiah" (called Christ) "is coming. When he comes, he will explain everything to us."[26] Then Jesus declared, "I, the one speaking to you—I am he" (NIV). The story changed in this way Jesus told her "you want the living water go and call your husband." The woman answered that she had no husband and Jesus told her that she was telling the truth even the man she had in her house was not her husband. Sometimes it's good to shame the devil, the woman was planning to take Jesus as a husband the way she did with other men. But then she was ashamed that He knew already who she was. I would love if men were like Jesus who sees things far and ready to defend yourselves. Men of today always have a backup plan I lost control. Control yourselves men and men know that a particular woman is seducing them but they always go for her but at the end they lie they lose control. Learn to shame the devil not because your married and you are keeping your commitment but because you fear the Lord your God. Learn to fear God.

You know what that woman was lucky; she wanted someone to tell how dirt she was so that she could clean her mess. Sometimes we need to work for the Lord through serving others. Many are out there looking and seeking for our help. Blaming someone will not help us to know their weakness but making them worse than before. We need to hold each other's hand to work with the Lord to save others out there. He died for us so that we can be saved, we need to go out there and preach the good news of the Lord to the World. We can see that the need of the woman was to be saved and after she was saved, she had no shame but to go and shout out there to preach about the Messiah, Jesus Christ. When we have Christ in our life will not be ashamed we will preach to everyone. Let us show the world that we are not the same they used to know us. You know what? Sin will never make us free, will always be the victims. If we want to be free people we need to have Christ, we will be saved and will have peace and courage.

CHAPTER THIRTEEN

He is My Shepherd

The Lord is my Shepherd: If you have God in you believe in Him, no matter what? Trust in the Lord. He is there with us in every situation we are in. He promised to be there for us. God shows us right paths always, we may feel pain because He always wants us to remember and respect every way we pass. Sometimes things get tough hence we experience more troubles time and again and you think God is not there. You ask yourselves as; why me? Why all this happening to me? Why God? But God do everything for our own good and His glory. Remember Job passed through the same, but at the end of it, there was restoration. The same pain you have, the more joy coming, let God restore and promote you in all situations you are in. Memorialize this chapter and wait for the Lord, welcome your blessings do not chase them away. Psalm 23: 1-6 The LORD IS MY SHEPHERD; I SHALL NOT WANT. [2] He maketh me to lie down in green pastures: he leadeth me beside the still waters. [3] He restoreth my soul: he leadeth me in the paths of righteousness for his name's sake. [4] Yea, though I walk through the valley of the shadow of death, I will fear no evil: for thou art with me; thy rod and thy staff they comfort me. [5] Thou preparest a table before me in the presence of mine enemies: thou anointest my head with oil; my cup runneth over. [6] Surely goodness and mercy shall follow me all the days of my life: and I will dwell in the house of the LORD FOR EVER.

HE IS ALWAYS BY MY SIDE

Psalm 32:8 King James Version (KJV)

I will instruct thee and teach thee in the way which thou shalt go: I will guide thee with mine eye. There was a certain lady who was travelling and it was her first time to use a flight and her first long flight. She was very young lady around 20 years of age. Initially, she was afraid and she was not sure where she was going to. At the airport she was given two boarding passes instead of three and she asked, "am I not supposed to have three boarding passes?" The one who was giving her boarding passes answered in a rude way, "hey! Many people never reach there, haven't you heard, you will come back very soon." This young lady smiled and finally she said "see you soon."

But the young lady was afraid and she went and told her Dad; "I can't make it," but her Father told her; "you have God my dear daughter and He will lead you and He is the one who planned your journey not me not your Mother, its God who did it." Then she left from her country. Finally, she got to her last stop to connect with another flight and the immigration asked her; where was her ticket. As I have already said that it was her first time travelling, so she looked at the policeman and smiled then told him where she was going. And the policeman took her to the office and to the other policeman and asked her again; "young lady where are you going?" She answered as before. And he kept on asking; "why do you have only two used boarding passes?" She said "I do not know sir."

You know what happened next, instead of returning home they just started working on her staff, searching where she bought her ticket and made a way for her as she was in transit. The two policemen helped her and she just passed the boarder without searching her again. In addition, she was given another boarding pass and told the air hostess to take a good care of her. If you have God and you believe and give everything to Him, you will pass anywhere. No matter how rude people are, you will make it. Luke 19:40 "I tell you," he replied, "if they keep quiet, the stones will cry out." With God there is always a way. No matter how they block you or close all doors, God will find a small hole and you will make it. God's secret is that no matter what the devil plans against you, He always has the way out for you.

IS IT WORTH

1 Thessalonians 5:18 King James Version

"In everything give thanks: for this is the will of God in Christ Jesus concerning you." In all things I just found out that there is no perfect person or hero, or anyone on top of the other on Earth. Why? Apply this verse in your life, the way you have passed until today, is it worth to say that its true I am supposed where I am today? Is it? It clearly tells us that in all circumstances give thanks, for it is God's will. Remember, to be somebody today, it's not your will, many tried but failed. For example; to be a president it is not because people voted or what they see in you. It is not because you are wise, they are many wise people more than you but God never keep them on top. Think of this, did we choose the home we are? Did we have an opportunity to choose parents, or did we choose children? They just come in our life as a gift? Did we choose to be born with disabilities? We choose to have disabilities when we were born? Did we choose to be orphans? Did we choose to be white or black or Asian or Indian? Did we choose to look the way we are now? We never choose to be what we are. Let me tell you whatever you are, there is no excuse to fail since we belong to God He who knows better that we do.

To be an orphan it's not an excuse to fail, being poor it's not an excuse, being a widow is not an excuse, being with a disability is not an excuse. Whatever you think is an excuse to your life rubs it now, take it out of your head. Take that as a gift of God and plan it with Him. God allows you to be poor, orphan, widow, disabled and many more, because you are strong. Whatever you are, just know that you are strong and God does not give us a burden. Even when someone laughs or tries to pull you down be firm you are worth just as they are. World is full of challenges so if we are busy, judging, controlling, make money for others, just know that you are lucky for God does not punish you. Sometimes we may think we are clever but we do not know that what we are sowing is what we will reap. What we do today will affect us in future.

We may be suffering because of our fathers if it is so, we may ask God to forgive us. Sometimes we may wonder that our family have problems one after another. God is love no matter how and why you are suffering. What we need to do is to surrender all to Him, Love the way you are and make more achievement with that. God let us succeed in everything so that we can understand that He never fails and He will never fail us. He is and He is there Alpha and Omega. Take Him or leave Him, He is still God and you cannot change that, and He is very powerful God, But He has everlasting love. We are safe in our daily activities because God is love. Without that I do not think that I would be able even to write his words today. God's love is greater does not look at how sinful we are that is why we are still breathing today and still receiving His blessing.

WHY DO WE USE GOD INSTEAD OF GIVING HIM AUTHORITY

The answer is simple we choose not to know Him. We choose to put God in our pocket and let Him out like money just as when we want to buy something. We use God when money cannot do it. Isaiah 52: 11 "Depart, depart, go out from there! Touch no unclean thing! Come out from it and be pure, you who carry the vessel of the Lord" (NIV). Sometimes I ask a question; since when did God change to be helper than the owner? We want God when we are stack. We need God when the world is at war but when we are making rules and laws do we include God? Do we ask God's guidance to allow abortion and homosexual marriages in our societies? But when we have nature problems, like death, volcano, flood, earthquakes and may more, we are busy asking questions why God, why me? God gives us emotions; so that we can know which is bad and which is good. But we choose to close eyes, nose, ears and feeling so that we cannot know what is good or bad. Let me tell you this story, there was a boy who was eating Guava, and it was at night and when he opened the inside of it and it was rotten. So this clever boy chose to eat the guava in dark so that he could not see inside of it. Many of us now choose to pretend that we are blind so as to avoid seeing. We hate the truth, we are afraid to lose our loved ones and we choose to cheat them. What are we doing people, why don't we use our body parts accordingly?

Hey! We have to be ashamed, look around, sex is powerful than love. Changing partners like clothes with no conscious is of no help. Testing each other like meat, grow up people. Indeed, God gives us test for a good purpose, we have to feel disgusted sometimes. We do not care at all and lying yourself that we are all going to die. Yes we will die but it's not an excuse to dig a pit and making a grave to ourselves. Stop blaming God and put a blame on ourselves and ask God for forgiveness, and then we can ask help. (What do you mean?) Accept faults and allow God control in our-lives, our home, our families, community, town, city, country and the world. Let us see how merciful and free we can be if we choose God alone. Bear in mind God is king of kings and He is coming very soon. Better to open eyes now than die with our choices. Salvation is for everyone indeed but it needs us to accept it. There is no righteous on earth not even one, but we are trying and we have to try every day to be righteousness. Let us hold hands to preach about salvation. He is on his way we better be ready.

DO WE KNOW THAT WE ARE THE IMAGE OF GOD

Do we know where we came from? Do we know our maker? Do we know why we are here? Do we know how unique we are in the presence of the Lord? All these questions I ask because I think we do not know ourselves. This is evident as nowadays people choose to be like animals 1Corinthians 6:13 Food for the stomach and the stomach for food.- but God will destroy them both. The body is not meant for sexual immorality, but Lord, and the Lord for the body. It can be silly but this is true, we are busy building our body like plants, for what? Just to be sexy. We love our bodies than what is inside. Thus; we love the outside than God. Look at yourself; women and men how many cosmetics do you use in your body? We spend a lot of money for plastic surgery while we see many people dying every day because of cancer. Why don't we use the same energy to work for everlasting life, where we will never grow old? Ladies feel happy when a man say you are sexy, while he wants to taste us like fish, meat, chicken, vegetables etc., we are happy to change partners. We are happy to use sex as greeting, people we have to respect God's things. Sex is gift that God gives us in a right time; it's a bond between married couples, not a greeting. Why don't you ask yourselves why God put it at the middle and hidden, made it to be much respected thing in our body? Why didn't God put it in the forehead so that we can use it anyhow? Let us respect the temple of the Lord. What do we think of our body? It's not a machine, stop making money using your body precisely, doing sex in the end getting paid. No excuses God did not fail to feed us, so that you can use your body as a money maker. Do not be a sex machine, sleeping with 100 men and women. Is that a thing that you can stand and be proud of? Let me tell you, it's a shame, very shameful thing. Use your energy with a brain and find something that you can be proud of. Sex brings a lot of pain on earth now; we can see many unfaithful marriages, children born without knowing their fathers, abortions, unwanted pregnancy, rape, diseases, divorce, orphan, family problems and many more. God is not happy with our behaviour and we need to respect God's gift. We need to ask God for forgiveness. Use God's things in the right manner and in the way He created it. Indeed, God is slow to anger and also a consuming fire. God wants to use our bodies because He is the one who created our bodies. We need to let God use our bodies in His own way and His glory.

CHAPTER FOURTEEN

Does God Speak to His People

Genesis 3:8-9 "Then the man and his wife heard the sound of the Lord God as he was walking in the garden in the cool of the day, and they hid from the Lord God among the tree of the garden.[9] But the Lord God called to the man Where are you?" (NIV) Apart from the sin, I just want us to see how God loves us and how He wants us to make a close relationship with Him. God speaks to us in many ways and He is always by our side. Although we are sinners He still comes and searches for us, as we can see in verse nine He asked where are you? God wants us to be close to Him, listen to Him and honour Him. In John 14; 15 "If ye love me, keep my commandments," (JKV). Jesus says we are his friend if we do what He commands. Suppose you have a friend but you never communicate, is there any friendship then? Or is just someone you know. God wants us to communicate with him, He wants us to have special time for Him and chart with Him. God wants us to have a strong relationship as He did with Elijah, Moses, Enoch, Mary, Joseph, Daniel, John, David, Peter, Samuel, Nehemiah, Joshua, Gideon and many more. Genesis 5:24 "Enoch walked with God: then he was no more, because God took Him away," (NIV). Enoch, man of God walked with God for 300 years without any sin and God had no reason to still keep Enoch on earth and He took Him away. Why can't we be like Enoch to live in the world of sin and never be like the world? We need to maintain our friendship with God. We have to give God our hearts and listen to Him.

ENOCH WALKED WITH GOD, DO WE WALK WITH GOD?

Genesis 5:24 "Enoch walked faithfully with God; then he was no more, because God took him away" (NIV). What is walking with? Does God have a right time to walk with? Walking with God is the most and powerful thing we need to do in our life as Christians. And God has no right time to walk with a person and He wants us to walk with him for the day we were born and ever. Have you ever walked with a friend going somewhere? When walking with someone, it needs two people walking side by side? The how do we walk with God? Do we let Him go in front of us or behind us? If we let God walk in front of us that means He will go away or we might be disturbed with other things and found out that God is gone. And if we let him walk behind us we will leave Him and find our own ways. Let us take God and walk by our side. Firstly, we need to walk with God in our mind, our heart, our faith and our body. If we let God guide our mind and our heart that means we are in a good way with Him. We need to take God in our ways, the way we talk let the spirit of God speak with us, the way we behave let God show His characters on us. God wants to walk with us where ever we go, do not take God when we are in trouble because that is not walking with God. Do not walk with God when you meet your church members or a pastor. Walk with God for the rest of your life.

Enoch took God to His working place he was never shy to talk about his God that is why God took Him to heaven without death. Some of us are ashamed to talk to others that we are Christians yet Enoch managed to do the opposite of what we do. He never forgot God because he was his first lover. To some of us God is our second option in life. Our parent, in-law, husband, wife, children, boss and many more are first in our lives than God. Sometimes we ignore God's power. Thus; we have some idols we believe in. Most of us fear people than God. If you put God first in everything like Enoch did our school will be easy, our marriage, work, our life will be best than ever. Students put God first in your life and you will see wonders. It happened to me when I was writing my A 'level examinations, I asked God to help me, and he did. The first day I dreamed the questions of the paper which I was going to write and when I was reading them I understood everything. Morning came and entered the examination room and found out that what I had dreamed was on the question paper. The next day I panicked because I never dreamed but I heard a voice saying "check that paper and that paper and see that number and that one". I told my friends to discuss the past examination paper and I also specified questions to be discussed. Upon entering the examination room we discovered that all questions which were discussed were the ones which appeared on the past question paper and my friends were surprised as to how I knew about the exact questions which were discussed were the ones appearing on the examination question paper. I told them that it was not me but God. If you make a relationship with God everything goes on perfectly well.

Make a relationship with God and make a strong communication with Him. One day my phone was ringing and I heard a voice "do not pick it up you are not ready." I took the phone should I answer it and the voice came again "do not answer that phone." I left it ringing; six times I never answered it. Suffice to say that it was anonymous call. Then another phone rung, and the same voice said unto me "pick that one." I pick it and the message was: "someone was calling you and you did not answer as such she is furious with what you have done to her? She is so angry with you, you should call her to say sorry" then I asked God "am I ready to call, what am I going to say?" God said unto me "call her and listen never say a word," I called her and said you called she just said I think the message was not yours. You can see how God works. There are situations which we need God to speak for us, fight for us and comfort us. All what God wants are people who can listen, obey and understand Him.

Enoch walked with God, if Enoch managed to walk with God what about us? Hebrews 11:5 "By faith Enoch was taken from this life, so that he did not experience death: he could not be found, because God had taken him away. For before he was taken, he was commanded as one who pleased God" (NIV). We need to please God we need to walk with God so that we can be one of the people who have faith in this world. I believe that Hebrews 11 is still writing in heaven and we will found our names there if we make it there. Do we please God in our day to day activities or is God pleased with us through our deeds? It's simple to live obedient life and have peace with God.

FIND GOD'S FAVOUR

Exodus 33:13-14 "Moses said to the LORD, "You have been telling me, 'Lead these people,' but you have not let me know whom you will send with me. You have said, 'I know you by name and you have found favour with me.' If you are pleased with me, teach me your ways so I may know you and continue to find favour with you. Remember that this nation is your people." The LORD replied, "My Presence will go with you, and I will give you rest," (NIV). Ask yourself "am I one of the God's favoured?" That answer will give us a light track to know where we are. Moses knew that he was one of important people in God's eyes. And because of that he also knew how powerful our God is. Then Moses asked God to teach him His words. Do we ask God to teach us? Many people are leaders in many ways, being a mother is a leadership, Father is leadership, Sister is leadership and brother leadership as well. We are leaders even in church, working places and every place people live there is a need for a leader. Although we are leaders, who guides us and teaches us to lead others? Where do we get authority from? Most of us we are the leader to our own life, do we let God teach and live in us. Do not forget God is Alpha and Omega; the beginning and the last and He is there always. God has more experience than we think and He knows our future and He knew us before we were born. Is there anybody wiser than Him?

Exodus 33: 17 "And the LORD said to Moses, "I will do the very thing you have asked, because I am pleased with you and I know you by name" (NIV). What a lovely answer from God, "I am pleased with you." Can God say to us that He is pleased after all evil things we do. There is a danger here I always ask myself; do we receive God's blessings because we are pleased with Him or because He is love? I hope this is the best question to each one of you. Do not forget He says He is the loving God and He allows rain and sun to rise and pour out respectively to every one of us, evil and good. And he allows evil plan works and in the end He destroys them. God wants us to be one of His favours. Let us bear in mind that Blessed are the ones who find favour in the Lord. Let us be one of them, and let God teach us. He is the only best teacher. If you want to know more, God is the key. The beginning of wisdom is to fear the Lord.

WHEN WE HAVE GOD
WE WILL BE GIVEN WHAT WE WANT

Where do we go when we are in trouble? Generally, the bible tells us what to do precisely 2 Kings 4:18-37 says [18] The child grew, and one day he went out to his father, who was with the reapers. [19] He said to his father, "My head! My head!"

His father told a servant, "Carry him to his mother." [20] After the servant had lifted him up and carried him to his mother, the boy sat on her lap until noon, and then he died. [21] She went up and laid him on the bed of the man of God, then shut the door and went out.

²² She called her husband and said, "Please send me one of the servants and a donkey so I can go to the man of God quickly and return."

²³ "Why go to him today?" he asked. "It's not the New Moon or the Sabbath."

"That's all right," she said.

²⁴ She saddled the donkey and said to her servant, "Lead on; don't slow down for me unless I tell you." ²⁵ So she set out and came to the man of God at Mount Carmel.

When he saw her in the distance, the man of God said to his servant Gehazi, "Look! There's the Shunammite! ²⁶ Run to meet her and ask her, 'Are you all right? Is your husband all right? Is your child all right?'"

"Everything is all right," she said.

²⁷ When she reached the man of God at the mountain, she took hold of his feet. Gehazi came over to push her away, but the man of God said, "Leave her alone! She is in bitter distress, but the LORD has hidden it from me and has not told me why."

²⁸ "Did I ask you for a son, my lord?" she said. "Didn't I tell you, 'Don't raise my hopes'?"

²⁹ Elisha said to Gehazi, "Tuck your cloak into your belt, take my staff in your hand and run. Don't greet anyone you meet, and if anyone greets you, do not answer. Lay my staff on the boy's face."

³⁰ But the child's mother said, "As surely as the LORD lives and as you live, I will not leave you." So he got up and followed her.

³¹ Gehazi went on ahead and laid the staff on the boy's face, but there was no sound or response. So Gehazi went back to meet Elisha and told him, "The boy has not awakened."

³² When Elisha reached the house, there was the boy lying dead on his couch. ³³ He went in, shut the door on the two of them and prayed to the LORD. ³⁴ Then he got on the bed and lay on the boy, mouth to mouth, eyes to eyes, hands to hands. As he stretched himself out on him, the boy's body grew warm. ³⁵ Elisha turned away and walked back and forth in the room and then got on the bed and stretched out on him once more. The boy sneezed seven times and opened his eyes.

³⁶ Elisha summoned Gehazi and said, "Call the Shunammite." And he did. When she came, he said, "Take your son." ³⁷ She came in, fell at his feet and bowed to the ground. Then she took her son and went out," (NIV).

We need to answer the question through this story, when the man saw that the son was sick, he said took him to the mother. The man knew that the child was a precious gift that God gave the woman for the kindness she showed to the man of God. When the woman had the son she took a good care as all mothers do but the son died. However, she never told anyone that her son was dead, she just went and followed that man of God. Do we know where to go with our problems or when we are in trouble? May be we report our problems to wrong people in the name of seeking attention or so that they may feel pity. We need to learn from this story that when you have problems find good solution(s) than talk about it. This woman on verse twenty six when Gehazi asked if she was alright, her husband and her child if were alright, she said everything was alright. Surely, she was very wise for she knew that Gahazi was not part of her solution. Look at us today when we are in trouble we become overwhelmed such that we tell everyone about it. Learn to keep quite sometimes, the devil always wait for the feedback. Thus; we might never know that by tell everyone we are giving him an update. We have to keep quite tell God alone and you can share afterwards as a testimony.

When the man of God saw the woman he saw that something went wrong and he asked his servant to welcome her. When the servant asked if she was alright, she responded that she was fine and continued going to the man of God. When the woman met the man of God she talked and accused the man of God, Elisha for giving her hope. Learn to give your problems to God because He is always there for us and when we are in such situations it's when He comes closer to listen to us. Do not let others make our problem viewed as a small thing while it hurts us. Know your problem and know where you can find a solution, if God gives hope He can solve it again. If you are going through problems talk to God and ask Him questions like what did Moses and Elijah do? And look at them today they are in paradise. Make a close relationship with God than any other person here on earth.

It needs mentioning that the woman knew that if God gave her a baby then He will bring the life back again. We need to know this if our things are not working well today. Do not waste time going to psychic, doctors, banks, cancelling and may more for solution. If that wife or husband brings trouble in your life do not cheat, do not divorce, do not run away ask God for solution. Run away if God says so, Divorce if God says so, do what God says because you will have peace and be free. Give God a chance to heal you, give him a chance to control the economy in your home, let Him reform and bring back all the loss.

If it comes from the Lord and there is a problem we need to thank God not to blame Him. Because God does everything for a purpose and let God amend and control all our needs. The child came back to life and the woman was happy again. When things turn upside down, we have to remain with God and see His goodness as the woman did. That is when she went back she never accepted the death of her child. In a way, she did not accept that death comes and it happens all the time. Although it had happened to many people she did not accept it as a result of her faith her son lived again. We need to do what this woman did until God gives us another chance with our lives. Do not say "well I am a sinner nobody can help me" know that it shall be well with God and everything God will overcome it.

THE WIDOW'S OFFERING

MARK 12:41-44

"Jesus sat down opposite the place where the offering were put and watched the crowd putting their money into the temple treasury. Many rich people threw in the large amount. But a poor widow came and put in two very small copper coins, worth only a fraction of a penny. Calling his disciples to him, Jesus said, I tell you the truth, this poor widow has put more into the treasury than all the others. They all gave out of their wealth: but she, out of her poverty, put in everything-all she had to live on." Do we know that giving is very important than receiving. Although it is like that what type of sacrifice do we do? Do we give to show off that we have more? Or do we give because we are tired of it or because it's too old or out of fashion for us? Give with all your heart feel good, in other words; give what you love most. What do we give God actually in church? Do we give God a change or we give God according to His blessing we receive in our dairy life. When you give, you will never be in lack. When you give with your whole heartedly, you will not count when you give or when you do something good to somebody. Whenever you are giving, give God and say I give it to you Lord. When you are giving something say I am giving my Father in heaven and forget that you gave. Let God give back not going to the same person say I want this because I helped you last time, you will be disappointed at the end. But when you are in need ask God and you can remind Him and wait for God alone to give it to you.

WHAT HAPPENS TO THE DEAD?

What happens when the person is dead? Do they go to heaven? What happens to their spirits? We may have so many questions about death due to our loved ones who are dead. Sometimes we ask ourselves if we are going to meet them. Ecclesiastes 9:4-6 "⁴For to him that is joined to all the living there is hope: for a living dog is better than a dead lion. ⁵For the living know that they shall die: but the dead know not anything, neither have they any more a reward; for the memory of them is forgotten. ⁶Also their love, and their hatred, and their envy, is now perished; neither have they any more a portion for ever in anything that is done under the sun" (NIV).

According to the verses above we have the true answer about death. They never know anything and they are gone. Everything about them is history. We can have a question sometimes as to why the dead come to us in dreams. And when we dream about them, we know that something good will happen to us. Sometimes when we dream about them, it is a disaster. But how come we dream about them yet the bible tells us that they do not know anything? Yes they never know everything, but sometimes are the evil spirits which join us in dreams. Sometimes it's God who appear to us. In other writings it is written that everyone has its own angel who guides him or her, when we are dead these angels are busy closing our case in many ways. For instance, if the death was done by killing, the angels work best to review the truth. God is at work, He is investigating our case always. God is righteous either ways because He reviews everything and He is always there watching. What do we do when we dream about our loved ones who are dead? Do we ask God to tell us what it is all about or we just make tea and forget? God's mysterious ways, He talks to us in many ways, any time, he uses any object as long as we understand Him. All we need to do is to seek help and understanding.

RESURRECTION

What will happen after the suffering of this world? What is our hope now? The answer is simple Jesus Christ rose from the dead that means we worn everlasting life after that incident. We were saved by Him. He promised us to come again and take us with Him to our home where our Heavenly father lives, where we will live for ever and ever. Yes one day will have everlasting life.1 Corinthians 15:20-28 [20] But Christ has indeed been raised from the dead, the first fruits of those who have fallen asleep. [21] For since death came through a man, the resurrection of the dead comes also through a man. [22] For as in Adam all die, so in Christ all will be made alive. [23] But each in turn: Christ, the first fruits; then, when he comes, those who belong to him. [24] Then the end will come, when he hands over the kingdom to God the Father after he has destroyed all dominion, authority and power. [25] For he must reign until he has put all his enemies under his feet. [26] The last enemy to be destroyed is death. [27] For he "has put everything under his feet." Now when it says that "everything" has been put under him, it is clear that this does not include God himself, who put everything under Christ. [28] When he has done this, then the Son himself will be made subject to him who put everything under him, so that God may be all in all"(NIV).

What will happen with our bodies? Surely, we are going to change our bodies to one spirit and we will know each other as well. In other writings it is written that all men will look like Adam and all women will look like Eve. In short will look as the way God wanted us to be in the first place when He said all is well. It will be lovely to change, if you have no legs, eyes, arms, hair, nose and anything we wish to have but due to other circumstances we do not have shall be restored on that day. Both the dead and the ones who will be alive by that time will change. 1 Corinthians 15:35-58 [35] But someone will ask, "How are the dead raised? With what kind of body will they come?" [36] How foolish! What you sow does not come to life unless it dies. [37] When you sow, you do not plant the body that will be, but just a seed, perhaps of wheat or of something else. [38] But God gives it a body as he has determined, and to each kind of seed he gives its own body. [39] Not all flesh is the same: People have one kind of flesh, animals have another, birds another and fish another. [40] There are also heavenly bodies and there are earthly bodies; but the splendour of the heavenly bodies is one kind, and the splendour of the earthly bodies is another. [41] The sun has one kind of splendour, the moon another and the stars another; and star differs from star in splendour.

[42] So will it be with the resurrection of the dead. The body that is sown is perishable, it is raised imperishable; [43] it is sown in dishonour, it is raised in glory; it is sown in weakness, it is raised in power; [44] it is sown a natural body, it is raised a spiritual body.

If there is a natural body, there is also a spiritual body. [45] So it is written: "The first man Adam became a living being"; the last Adam, a life-giving spirit. [46] The spiritual did not come first, but the natural, and after that the spiritual. [47] The first man was of the dust of the earth; the second man is of heaven. [48] As was the earthly man, so are those who are of the earth; and as is the heavenly man, so also are those who are of heaven. [49] And just as we have borne the image of the earthly man, so shall we bear the image of the heavenly man. [50] I declare to you, brothers and sisters, that flesh and blood cannot inherit the kingdom of God, nor does the perishable inherit the imperishable. [51] Listen, I tell you a mystery: We will not all sleep, but we will all be changed— [52] in a flash, in the twinkling of an eye, at the last trumpet. For the trumpet will sound, the dead will be raised imperishable, and we will be changed. [53] For the perishable must clothe itself with the imperishable, and the mortal with immortality. [54] When the perishable has been clothed with the imperishable, and the mortal with immortality, then the saying that is written will come true: "Death has been swallowed up in victory."

⁵⁵ "Where, O death, is your victory? Where, O death, is your sting?"

⁵⁶ The sting of death is sin, and the power of sin is the law. ⁵⁷ But thanks be to God! He gives us the victory through our Lord Jesus Christ.

⁵⁸ Therefore, my dear brothers and sisters, stand firm. Let nothing move you. Always give yourselves fully to the work of the Lord, because you know that your labour in the Lord is not in vain" (NIV).

Let us keep our faith in the Lord our God. One day we shall live with Him together, we will ask all questions we wanted to know. We will live together without parting again we will live as one, one family of God. Imagine we will meet again and meet new people. Pray for that day so that we can be one of them when we will listen and talk our experience we have been in here on earth. My dear beloved friends we need to make it to heaven, we have to be there and know each other like seeing the same faces we saw on earth and celebrate for our victory.

THE NEW JERUSALEM

1Peter4:12-14 "Dear friends, do not be surprised at the painful trial you are suffering, as though something strange were happening to you. But rejoice that you participate in the suffering of Christ, so that you may be overjoyed when his glory is revealed if you are insulted because of the name of Christ, you are blessed, for the spirit of glory and of God rest on you" (NIV). Peter comforts us that any suffering we meet we should rejoice. It is not easy to rejoice when we are suffering.

My friend had many problems which followed one after another. Thus; her children were on foster care, the government refused to give her kids, separation with a husband, falling sick and looking for help to come home and her relative told her that they could not afford to buy a ticket for her and kids. I used to ask myself; why was she having more trials? Why was this happening to a faithful woman like her who is one of the strongest followers of Christ? Indeed that overnight I had a vision in which I was told that she was getting thin because of troubles and I asked God why He was showing me this instead of helping her. God answered me that I should pray for her so that she should pass through. The answer was not enough for me until I opened my bible and read 1 peter 4 "all we need to rejoice because we are blessed." And I laughed and said may be this suffering will be our history in heaven. Consequently, it will lead us to heaven because as Christians when we are in problems, it is when we need to leave close to God.

There are some other people who never suffer. It is very doubtful if such people their Christian life will grow. When others are insulting because of the name of Christ that means the spirit and the glory of God rests on us hence, we are not like any other person. Such being the case, we need to do here on earth is to be instructed by the authority of heaven. When we go by what our heavenly father wants, the devil is not happy as a result he wants to deal with us. God allows us to suffer because Christ himself suffered but He overcame sin. God wants us to overcome sin and he wants us to prove to the world how good He is. When we are suffering with Christ we have faith that we shall overcome someday. And the spirit of the Lord comforts us all the way and others may see us like we are suffering but we have joy of the Lord. If Christians were living very happy in this world, would we remember that this world is not our home and we are passing by? Trials work as bells in our lives reminding us that soon we are going home. Make your suffering today as ringing bell that Christ is calling us home and we need to live here in this earth as visitors. This is evident in the bible precisely in Revelation 21:1- 4 And I saw a new heaven and a new earth: for the first heaven and the first earth were passed away; and there was no more sea. ² And I John saw the holy city, New Jerusalem, coming down from God out of heaven, prepared as a bride adorned for her husband. ³ And I heard a great voice out of heaven saying, Behold, the tabernacle of God is with men, and he will dwell with them, and they shall be his people, and God himself shall be with them, and be their God. ⁴ And God shall wipe away all tears from their eyes; and there shall be no more death, neither sorrow, nor crying, neither shall there be any more pain: for the former things are passed away (KJV).

Heaven is the place where will be no more sin because everything on it will be new. We will live with God and He will be our God. God will assure us that we will be with Him forever and ever. I like verse four that God will wipe our tears, no more mourning or crying or pain or death all older things have passed away. I refer 1 peter 4 says we should rejoice when we are suffering because God Himself will wipe our tears and they will be no more death, pain, crying and mourning. Cry today because God Himself will wipe our tears and He will end all sinful nature and we will live happier ever after. Jesus is coming very soon and we need to prepare to meet Him and live with Him for ever and ever. Have your question to ask Elijah, Enoch, Moses, Abraham and many more. We will live with God and see Him as He is all the time. What a beautiful day will that be? Indeed we will say like Paul "I have fought a good fight, I have finished my course, I have kept the faith," (2 Timothy 4:7).